MW00929660

FREE MEXICAN AIRFORCE
WILL BE FLYING TONIGHT

The trials and tribulations of procuring,

transporting and selling marijuana

Terry Canipe

Copyright © 2017 Terry Canipe

All rights reserved. No part of this book may be reproduced, scanned, or redistributed in any printed or electronic form without prior, written permission of the author

Contents

Prologue

What makes a boy from a comfortable middle class family, in a time of economic prosperity for the United States, become a drug smuggler and live a life chasing danger? This book takes you on a journey of adventure, danger, and personal revelation.

Growing up in small town Texas I lived a solidly middle class life. In the late '50's and early '60's life was simple and easy for a young boy. While I am sure I was properly brought up, for the times, I had a freedom that may seem neglectful to today's parents. For example, I was driving trucks by age fourteen, overloaded lumber trucks, with cops turning a blind eye.

I always had the gift of the gab and the ability to bend others to my will, including authority figures. Add to that a sense of the bigger picture, even at such a young age and you have a budding entrepreneur. I had a taste of the thrill of rebellion at fourteen, when I got my first car and drove thirty miles to the county line to make a deal with the only liquor store in the area. Each week I bought anywhere between one and three hundred dollars worth of liquor - a lot of money in those days when the average yearly income was $5315.00 - which I resold. The legal age was twenty-one and I am sure I looked nowhere near that, but they didn't care. That was when I learned that profits come before compliance with the law. That lesson was an important one for all my life choices thereafter.

In 1967 I was drafted and immediately joined the Marine Corp Reserves, where I became a crack shot. I smuggled drugs for five of my six years in the Reserves, risking jail in a federal prison. I was good at it, and perfected the skill of looking the part of a good old boy with my hair cut Marine style and wearing a welder's hat. In that era, possibly still, that look is almost guaranteed to make you blend into the background, although in my case I looked scary, even to me!

The Vietnam War was a dark time in our history. I lost all respect for my government over that war, which has been called a proxy war. A proxy war, in essence, is a war between two parties where neither directly confronts the other. In that time nuclear conflict was looming between the Soviet Union and the United States, and a war like Vietnam was their way of fighting indirectly. It was never about Vietnam. The Soviet Union and other communist allies supported North Vietnam and the United States and allies supported South Vietnam. This war dragged on for twenty years.

I had done some protesting against the war in Vietnam and for Civil Rights and Women's rights. I lost friends I grew up with in the war and the ones who returned were forever changed and not for the better. They were treated as criminals and had a difficult time adjusting. Some were unable to make that adjustment, as they were not offered sufficient assistance from the government or the general public. In those days, the terrible mental price paid by those soldiers was largely unknown and untreated. Those men suffered, misunderstood and mistreated.

I decided to make my stand, to undermine my government in my own way and began smuggling drugs on a larger scale, not to make money, but to make a statement. The first poundage I helped smuggle sold for thirty-five dollars a pound. Of course I was past that at this point but still I was not thinking about money. I guess it was a romantic idealism I felt, to stick it to my government by smuggling a plant. There was the lure of adventure – and by now I was an adventure junkie – and I enjoyed pitting my wits against unknown adversaries. It was a life on the move, a life unfettered by the constraints of a regular nine to five job.

I still do not fully understand why I could be imprisoned for life for crossing an invisible line with a plant that could grow wild almost anywhere.

In my world it is a medicine!

The group I wanted to be connected to was small and secretive, as you can imagine. This has to be one of the hardest jobs to apply for on the planet. They looked for experience and reputation and the major problem was how to get the experience and build a log book based on reputation and experience.

How did I get that experience? Read on, it's a wild ride.

Chapter One

Marijuana can be used to treat and prevent the eye disease glaucoma, by decreasing the pressure inside the eye

Free Mexican Air Force

I may not have had much experience, but I had assets that couldn't be bought or taught and which saved my life on more than one occasion. This may be a career choice that appears, at first glance, to be best suited to someone with no fear or no other choice, someone who is more brawn than brains. This is not the case.

I have always been a planner. I don't make just a plan A, I make plan B and C as well. If plan A fails, and in my career that happened more often than I care to think about, I have fall back plans which have ensured my continued survival, and success.

I have motivation and determination. Once I begin I do not stop, mentally or physically. A moving target is hard to hit when you're in the field, and that's the logic which applies when setting up operations – keep them changing. Planning skills, organization, flexibility - those are attributes you can't buy.

My main enemy was incompetence in my chosen or unknown partners – those shadowy figures with whom connections were made while working out deals.

Incompetence in my enemies or rivals, on the other hand, was an asset to exploit.

I had one other asset more valuable than all the others. I had a sixth sense, a touch of magic inherited from my mother who always knew everything about me. Somehow I knew when things would go wrong, could sense disaster looming, could tell when someone was about to double cross me. My compatriots called me Radar because of this. Call it what you will, sixth sense, guardian angel, spirit companion. Whatever it was, without it I don't believe I would be here to tell these tales. That and a huge dose of luck.

***

My first action was in the late sixties, working on the Rio Grande river, where I did between two and five trips a year. A stretch of the Rio Grande acts as the border between Mexico and the United States and I swam or rafted large bales of marijuana, totaling 100-800 pounds per trip, from one country to another. This was exotic to me, and frankly exhilarating. I became an adventure junkie, loving the surge of adrenalin that accompanies danger and the rush that accompanies success.

This was where my attributes as a leader – clear, concise thinking and incisive decision making – showed and made me someone others looked to for viable, useful suggestions on what to do and how to do it. One aspect of being a leader in a potentially lethal situation is to accept that role if it is given to you. People living a dangerous life know who to trust. False modesty will get you killed.

That river was spooky to say the least with all kinds of shaking going on. Just about anything was smuggled, day and night, during my time. I have no doubt it continues to this day. One example of this: During a small volume marijuana crossing I saw another group smuggling rocking chairs, about a hundred of them. They were in the same area as me and my crew, and of course me seeing them meant they could see me. Such close proximity leads to paranoia for all.

Because several crews I didn't know used the same area as me I felt compelled to search out a new spot. This led to the only real trouble I experienced on this stretch of river.

My crossing partner Chico was a long term, trusted friend. He was taking me to inspect a new crossing point in southern Texas. The main man in the area was Gringo, and I knew the Mexicans who worked for him very well. The Mexicans would cross the product then walk two to five miles carrying the weed and deliver it to several different stash houses. The next day you would pick it up and take it out of the valley. All the crossing people were unarmed with the exception of the Gringo. He had an M-16 with over 200 rounds, all in clips.

When Chico and I arrived there was a crossing underway, with about two thirds of the product crossed. The Gringo, a deserter from the army, did not like me being there. Vietnam was just too much for him and he was an unpredictable man at best. I am sure he suffered from PTSD but in those days it was not recognized. I often wonder how many men like Gringo were the result of that war. But I digress. The Gringo lived close to the river in Mexico. My crossing crew stated that he did not pay the basic rate or in full and was not respected.

I walked up and the Gringo threatened me with an automatic rifle. I, like the rest, was unarmed. Slowly, I turned my back to the irritated Gringo, letting him inspect and see that I carried no weapons. I jokingly said, "We are here now, everyone cool their jets. I am not a cop or a snitch. Just here looking at the possibility for future endeavors. Point that weapon in a different direction or use it. If not, you will get a surprise." Chico backed me and had position on the Gringo. He was unaware and frankly just posing/playacting, asshole.

Timing is everything in life whether it is planned or not. What happened next was not planned!

All hell broke loose as about eight bandits – definitely not cops - opened up with pistols. They only shot at the Gringo. About four on either side of the river emptied their pistols in him. I crawled over to the Gringo and saw he was gone, then took the M-16 and ammo and started firing back. I am a Marine trained, expert marksman. At every muzzle flash I put about half a clip on that spot. In short order they stopped firing.

A hush filled the air, nothing moving or making a sound, the air full of the smell of cordite.

I kept the crew from scattering and stood guard while they made backpacks containing 60-80 pounds of marijuana and we left in an organized hurry. The bandits did not follow – maybe they were all dead. I didn't stop to find out.

As they walked, the crossing crew talked amongst themselves in Spanish, remarking how lucky it was I had been there on this most unusual and dangerous crossing.

The next day I turned the load over to its owners. I thought they would appreciate two thirds of their load back and the location of their dead partner and friend. Not so, they accused me of orchestrating the whole thing. Obviously amateurs, which I was, too. This shocked me because it had never crossed my mind that I could keep it all. Why give up two thirds when you could keep it? I was left with threats in my wake and my only reward, puzzlement.

This was the catalyst that moved me out of south Texas.

***

I decided to move on, but applying for a job in my line of work in the interior of Mexico was a problem. It was word of mouth or reputation and I had only one person on my list, Gordo. I didn't realize it then, but Gordo was a poor choice.

On introduction I had ten minutes to convince him I was a good bet. Gordo's demeanor was aloof, bored, condescending and superior. He was hungover, had a raging headache and a cloudy memory of last night's debauchery. He was not in the mood for an interview.

Gordo thought I was too young and inexperienced for the job. I countered with my short list of accomplishments: A Marine, truck mechanic, and a commercial pilot – plus, balls, a vital ingredient in my opinion.

I did not know at the time that Gordo lacked them.

The pilot comment convinced him and two months later he called and invited me to Guadalajara.

My adventure junkie story really began at this point.

I was hired to do a river crossing in the Big Bend National park of Texas. It consisted of me driving a four wheel drive pick-up truck with a winch on the front across the Rio Grande. It sounded easy and relatively safe. I was to wade across the river with the winch cable checking for holes and large rocks, tie the cable to a large tree or rock, and then make the cross. Easy, especially after what I had been running into in south Texas.

Read on to discover just how wrong I was.

***

We left for Guadalajara with three men - me, Flaco, and Gordo - and one impressive woman, Jo. Within a couple of months she was to prove her worth. They took my Rambler to use as a point car. It was a six cylinder with no frills.

This was my first trip deep into México and I feel like a kid on Christmas morning. On that first trip I spoke very little Spanish. First words learned were fill the tank, please, then eggs and the check.

We arrived in Gaud and started shopping for our load. Absolutely nothing was available. We searched for ten days, no luck. Flaco's girlfriend Erin was already in the city when we arrived so our little band now consisted of three men and two women. Erin wanted to take a beach trip and pushed hard for it, an irony I have never learned to appreciate. We chose Tenacatita, close to Bara de Navidad in the state of Colima and about two hundred miles south of Guad.

Access to Tenacatita in those days was a dirt road, and we ended up in a large coconut plantation that ran for miles in most every direction except for the ocean. There were no buildings, only three grass palapas, simple open sided buildings with thatched roofs. The nearest telephone was over an hours drive away, remembering that this was the days before mobile phones. All we had was drinking water. The local Indians came to cook for us and made what could be called a windfall, unexpected and much appreciated money from us. We were happy too – we got wonderful food.

This beach was protected by a peninsula and was beautiful. The waves were small and great for swimming.

As the first to arrive we pitched camp, waiting for medical students from Guad who were coming to join us. We drove about four miles to another unprotected beach in order to watch the sunset. This beach was the total opposite to the first one and directly open to the ocean. The waves were much larger, over ten feet when they broke. The beach itself was like no other I have ever seen, with hills and valleys due to a recent storm. If you stood in a sand valley and someone was in the next over they were hidden from sight. The waves rolled in and stopped, sucking up the previous wave, building to ten plus feet and crashing down, throwing small rocks and making sand. There were mountains of sand up and away from the water line. This is called a beach break.

When we were there a fresh water river was dammed up by this sand. It only breaks through during the rainy season. I assume this is the case today, but things change. My group used this fresh water source to bath in as well as boil for a relatively clean water supply.

Apart from the beach there was a large airstrip I was interested in, big enough for a DC-3. We found a graveyard with around one hundred graves. No buildings to be seen. The airstrip was laid out parallel to the beach, producing a strong crosswind for any future landings or take-offs. The on shore breeze was brisk and would present a challenge to any pilot landing or taking off.

It was the middle of nowhere.

On the evening it happened we were excited about a special event, with the sun setting down the beach to our right and a full moon rising to our left. Very heavy tides!

We were in over our heads and did not have a clue.

At dusk we split up and started gathering wood for a fire.

Flaco's girlfriend, Erin, the one who pushed for this trip, was maybe fifty yards from me, kicking along in the foam at the top of the wave footprint. She was wearing shorts and a shirt, her purse over her shoulder, not even thinking of going in the water.

A large wave came from nowhere and she was suddenly knee deep in this churning mass. As the wave retreated the rip current pulled her down the slope toward the next wave. Flaco was on the other side of her and almost as far from her as I was. He saw this happening and sprinted towards her, yelling at her to move her feet. She didn't move, just let the wave pull her toward the bottom of the valley. The year before Flaco almost drowned there so he knew the danger. Erin was skiing toward massive trouble with a large smile. She did not understand what was happening, holding her purse, sliding backwards and smiling.

The ten foot plus wave smashed her, knocking her unconscious. Flaco reached her before the second wave hit and tried to keep her face out of the water. I was a trained lifeguard but I had no experience with anything remotely like this. In the apex of the wave the water was less than three feet deep but the current was so strong it was barely possible to stand alone, much less support someone unable to help. A rip current can pull even a strong swimmer out to sea. An unconscious person stands no chance.

A huge wave came in and they both disappeared. It moved Flaco thirty plus feet to our left and deposited him on one of those hills, totally spent. We reached him and pulled him up out of danger or he would have drowned also. We never saw Erin again.

Just ten seconds of carelessness cost Erin everything.

Flaco, Jo, Gordo and I were struck dumb. We did not speak about Erin. We sat on the tailgate of the truck and stared out at the ocean.

A breath-taking sunset and an equally impressive moonrise happened in quick succession as we sat on the back of the truck saying nothing. Horror and shock were all we were left with.

***

Around midnight a car pulled up and two men and one woman got out. They were very drunk and well armed with pistols and a machine gun. This startled our party into action. We had two pistols well hidden but they would do us little good where they were.

Sitting on the truck with the two noise makers we saw a van pulling up, one of the medical students looking for us. We had been missing for eight or more hours.

I told the story quickly to the student and he decided to go talk to the armed Mexicans.

It turned out they were Federal cops out trying to fuck the female and probably do some drunken shooting. We stupidly thought the student reported the death to the authorities. They did not report anything to anybody. There was no body, no proof that what we said happened or not so the cops couldn't care less.

***

We searched for Erin for over a month, with a boat and a motorcycle plus renting an airplane.

After a few days I figured all we might find was a part of her, as sharks roamed these waters, but it wasn't to be. There were many sharks of all sizes. I had done body recovery in a lake in Texas and had some idea of the extreme difficulty involved with the handling of a decomposed person so in a way, felt it was better there was no body to be recovered.

I was deeply concerned about Flaco's mental condition. Flaco was a trusted, good, dependable friend, a man of his word who lived his life accordingly. A man who could and did deliver on promises made, completely bankable. He was imprisoned and did nothing to his associates to shorten his sentence. He was an artist and saw the world from that perspective.

I did everything I could to lighten his load, but how can you lighten a load such as that?

Flaco stayed very drunk for the rest of the trip.

***

After searching for that very long month we needed a release from the incredible pressure we were under. Manzanillo was a little over an hour away. A medium small Mexican town it had a local Indian Festival taking place on the coming weekend. We decided to go, drinking beer on the way, and the further we got away from Tenacatita the drunker and more relaxed we became. It was just Flaco and me on this decompression trip. We bought Tequila and rum with almost no chasers to cut the lethal effects so we could reach our goal fast - totally numb with alcohol.

The day was beautiful and the costumes worn by the local Indian tribes colorful and a welcome escape from our search responsibilities. We were dangerously drunk and vulnerable due to the degree of inebriation. Worse for wear, we needed to leave for Tenacatita before sunset.

Leaning on each other we staggered to my car, obviously very impaired. As we reached the car we were surrounded by a one hundred plus gang of kids. In Mexico during this decade it was a common method for the local children to take advantage of drunken strangers. They surrounded the soon to be victims in a boll shaped formation with the younger children inboard and the older outboard. Jewelry, cameras, purses, hats, watches, anything they could sell would disappear into a sea of hands and arms not connected to a discernible body.

We were next to my car and Flaco had put one of our pistols in the glove compartment before we left Tenacatita. He tried to get into the car in a panic because we could do nothing to make our escape. He opened the glove compartment and grabbed the gun, but fell backward on the side of the car, waving the pistol high through the air while attempting to place it in his belt. This changed everything in the blink of an eye. All the kids disappeared like spit on a hot griddle. I was amazed, we went from victims to just drunk tourists in a nano second. It was a regrettable situation that fortunately played out in a fashion where no one was hurt.

We returned to the beach without any other drama. I have never pulled a stunt anything like that again to this day. I do learn from my mistakes.

**

Flaco taught me the do's and don'ts of smuggling marijuana. He was a wise mentor and I soaked up everything he taught me.

After we looked for that month Flaco was driven to call Erin's father and try to notify him that his daughter was no more. From this point on, Flaco and I were together most of the time till the end of this horrible event. I was in the room when Flaco made the call to Erin's father and tried to explain what had transpired.

Try to put yourself in that man's place. All he heard was a stranger in México telling of his daughter's death. We had no body, nothing but a beach to show him.

What would you think if you were he?

Flaco pleaded for her dad to come, all expenses paid, and go to the beach and just talk.

He didn't come but did send an uncle or a brother. I found out later he was a sick man and could not make the trip. The uncle or brother came, but did not talk to Flaco. He went to the police and at their insistence filed a warrant for Flaco's arrest for murder. No proof of anything except she was missing.

Any warrant for murder in México is fought from jail with about two years of your life and in most cases substantial amounts of money.

Fortunately for Flaco, Gordo, Jo, and I were with him when he was arrested. Gordo's lady Jo had a dog with her, a Doberman. That dog sat across me and kept the cops from busting me. I had five or six shake joints in my pocket and needed time to eat them.

We were taken into custody and gave our statements just the way it happened. That is the only thing that kept Flaco from doing thirty years for Erin's murder.

A Mexican jail in those days was not the place where a person was innocent until proven guilty. Nor was it a place where prisoners were treated fairly. They beat my ass pretty badly the second night and threatened me with five years for withholding information or thirty years as an accomplice. I was handcuffed to a chair bolted to the floor. The cops used phone books and other heavy instruments to beat me senseless. Nothing had sharp edges so as not to leave any lasting evidence that a beating had occurred. They had been torturing Flaco with electricity. He was tied to four metal posts cemented to the water covered floor of a concrete room, connected to a cord that plugged into a wall socket. The juice is not regulated at three in the morning. The voltage is so high light bulbs pop and crackle.

They told me to change my statement or I was going down with Flaco.

The only proof they claimed to have was a drawing Flaco did to deal with the reality of what happened – remember, he was an artist. It was a lifelike rendering of two figures in that apex of the wave. The wave had a monster face and claw like tendrils reaching up on the beach. He was holding her bent and lifeless body with one arm and shaking a fist at the wave with his other.

The police said he was beating her to death. This was their only so called proof. They thought he had been broken and would confess. I stated that I would not change my statement unless Flaco told me to. That caused them to bring Flaco to me.

I have never seen a person that white and still conscious. He couldn't walk, and no one spoke English to him. I quickly ran down the situation to him and Flaco started to deny what they were saying. They dragged him out and continued his torture.

Meanwhile, Gordo and his girlfriend Jo were not being tortured, luckily. His lady was in possession of our money to score the pot. She stuffed all our money into her vagina.

Very gutsy!

Without her cool, calm action our trip would have ended then and there. I wished that Jo was a partner instead of Gordo.

They also still had those two pistols, more on them a little later.

If you are ever in trouble in Mexico do not demand to see the American consulate. They will do absolutely nothing except inform your relatives. They will make an appearance to verify you are an American citizen and still above ground. The Consulate will present you with a stack of ancient Time magazines and Newsweek. Why they do this is puzzling. What help these magazines represent I do not know.

This was a murder charge and very serious. Nothing useful was offered, like a lawyer or any sort of representation. We were left alone to figure out what, if any, rights we had, or not. Mexican law is cloudy to say the least. Every charge is structured around bribery and how the Mexicans can justify the highest fines possible for any infraction.

After all this crap they finally decided there was no evidence. The Mexican cops hit us with a fine, which meant a bribe. Only eight hundred dollars, the price of a life, apparently. They did not need to justify the fine, why, I do not totally understand. I guess a mordida/bribe is normal procedure and is expected by everyone involved. If you travel to the third world and have a legal or illegal problem this is the only way it will be resolved.

Strange story, but this is what happened. We were very lucky to slide through this drama with only basically minor damage done plus losing eight hundred of our buying power. Poor Erin was the only true loser, and she paid with her life for a few seconds lack of focus. In comparison, we couldn't complain.

The cops found the two pistols. That could be five years apiece for the four of us. The cops started the negotiation and made threats to sentence us all to four or five years in the local sewer laughingly called a jail.

Flaco, Jo, Gordo and I had no counter to any charges the Mexican cops chose to file on us.

Gordo's lady Jo came through again. She was beautiful, and said her father insisted she be protected in México, therefore, the pistols were needed. With very little discussion, the cops agreed and gave one of them back to her. Who can tell what goes on in a Mexican cop's mind?

***

The story is not over. You're wondering where it will end? So was I.

We left and went to a town known for bad pot, Mazatlán, scored the second day there and left for Saltillo.

We were now three months into this insane trip. We left Gordo's lady with the pot in Saltillo and headed to the Big Bend in my Rambler. The rainy season had started which meant problems.

The immediate problem was the lack of a real road to Boquillas, just a creek bed, around one hundred and twenty miles of it, at ten miles an hour. It took a full day to get there. Boquillas is just south of the Texas border below the Big Bend National park. There was almost no traffic on this totally unimproved cat scratch of a road. How it was even used during the rainy season was a mystery to me. This was a road that would punish you and your vehicle severely.

We arrived late in the afternoon and found the river raging, having broken its banks. The river water was white with froth and unsuitable for our purpose and it would be one or two months until it was usable again.

Now Gordo's screw ups came into focus. He did this crossing about six or seven months before. He was falling down drunk. We discovered that was the only way he could work. He was lost and too drunk to figure it out, so he went to the only Cantina in town and hired a local to get him to the river at a place shallow enough to make the crossing.

Gordo paid that guy a few hundred and went to Texas.

Gordo never told Flaco or me about this unprofessional crossing and the attention he had brought to this crossing site.

The guy he hired talked about it in the Cantina. The local cops were waiting for Gordo's return. On that side of the river were maybe two hundred people in a fifty square mile area. Everyone stood out.

I pulled Flaco aside and asked, "What are we going to do about this loose cannon? He has put all of us in extreme danger. We have no escape route that is feasible and can see the cops obviously checking us out." There was very little time to make a plan and the river was clearly not swimmable.

The cops saw Flaco, Gordo and I looking at the rain swollen river. They recognized Gordo from the description given by the local he hired. The river was not passable, too dangerous.

There was no way I could do the trip for probably another two months.

The cops came over and said, "Follow us," for a questioning session.

We were fresh from the traumatic experiences in Guad and in no mood to talk to more cops so we chose to run. My Rambler six cylinder was the only choice for a getaway car. This region is desert, everything has thorns. We should have tried to swim the river but didn't.

We headed back down that cat scratch of a road at thirty to fifty miles an hour on a less than ten mile an hour road.

The cops followed in an army truck going a little slower. Flaco, Gordo and I made it forty or fifty miles. The car had no gas showing on the gauge since the tank had a hole in it. We topped a rise, got airborne, and blew two tires in the same instant.

It was about half way to the paved road and we were stranded, as well as being pursued by the army and the police. It just gets better, doesn't it?

We struck off on foot at a ninety degree angle to the road and got around a mile before the cops arrived at the car. We were out of the frying pan and into the fire.

Have you ever wondered how you would survive if you found yourself in the wilderness? How would you defend yourself against predators? What would you eat? Where would you find water?

The first night we saw in the distance a large thunderstorm. While walking in a creek like depression we were knocked off our feet by a short wall of water, maybe knee high.

It was full of desert trash, everything with thorns. This turned out to be a good thing because we had some water to drink out of puddles for the next three days. Otherwise we would have died. Flaco, Gordo and I walked our cowboy boots to pieces. I would guess seventy to one hundred miles in circles. We were covered in wounds from head to toe from all the thorny stuff we went through.

No one had a compass or a container to carry water and not one bite of food. It was very poor planning considering how remote and void of anything to sustain a human it was. This area is very sparsely populated, mostly small mining operations and even smaller cattle operations. It takes many acres to support even one cow.

As you may imagine, the mood of our three would-be smugglers had bottomed out and anger at Gordo for not telling of his problems on the last trip was surfacing.

Bickering built with the hunger and thirst. Gordo was a whiny, fat draw on what little energy was left. We were all wearing cowboy boots, not suited for those rough conditions.

Finally, we stumbled onto a small ranch where I had the very best meal of my life.

It consisted of a small pot of cold beans and a stack of tortillas that were going to the hogs. I hope never to have a better one. The ranchers, a small family, give us a corn crib to sleep in that was also very pleasant.

The next morning when we woke there was a pick-up truck in the yard. The man driving it saw us and recognized us, the three Gringos. The army was all over the area looking for us, checks about every ten miles on that very poor road. The truck driver said, "Come with me and I will get you around the checks and out to a road where you can catch a bus." What other cards did we have to play? Flaco, Gordo and

I went and he kept his word, driving around the army checks and putting us on a bus.

The pure substance displayed by the Mexican people has always astounded me. They are truly a great people!

We were almost totally broke and had nothing to offer the truck driver for his brave assistance. He did not even ask. We pooled what little we had and gave him less than one hundred dollars.

***

All this time Gordo's lady was sitting five plus days by herself with the load, holding her water, the trip obviously still screwed up. We needed another crossing.

I, much earlier than I was comfortable with, was the one setting up the new crossing, my first aircraft short out of México. Problem number one was I needed an on-load strip near Saltillo. I found a semi-useable one less than fifty miles from town.

That found, I traveled to Texas and rented an aircraft suitable for our purpose, also putting together a catch strip in central Texas and hiring people to do the off-load. All these preparations took another two weeks plus.

Because the load was less than one hundred and fifty miles deep into Mexico and the catch strip was south of San Antonio, I could make the trip on the available fuel on board the rented aircraft which meant no need for refueling in Mexico.

***

I made the crossing, flying at fifty feet above ground level, dodging power lines and water towers plus barns and grain storage units. It was successful and we were finally paid.

After all that my pay for the four plus months of my life being risked was less than seven thousand dollars. My car was worth half that.

But my reputation was made.

I had all the work I could do for the foreseeable future. I was in high demand and was respected as someone who would never quit and could be trusted.

As dumb as I was, I went right back six weeks later.

I did this kind of work for several decades. Adventure is as addictive as the finest drug. I am still hooked.

Chapter Two

Cannabis can be used to control seizures in epilepsy and decreases the seizures in Dravet's Syndrome

Guadalajara

You may be wondering if I was insane to come back to this place. The thing is, I had a taste of a different lifestyle and I liked it. I don't believe we are born to work, pay bills and die. We are born to experience life and, for me, the edge of danger gave life a sharper focus. Of course, like any job there were dull moments, and lighter times. The danger is always there but humans are not built to live in a permanent state of danger – it's too debilitating to the body. Everyone needs to relax, to take some time out.

The following story is an example of the lighter side to my job.

***

Flaco became my trainer and taught me how to package our product, marijuana, for the various methods of transportation used. The marijuana was compressed for ease of transportation and I helped design and build a press for this purpose.

We knew an imaginative and inventive mechanic in Austin who did top shelf work and whose designs were the best for our purposes. He used a large steel I beam, one that weighed over one hundred pounds, and cut it into sections. He formed a square box shape and welded it tightly. The box sat upright with a flat quarter inch piece of steel welded to the bottom of the press. A heavy duty wooden box built to the size of the package was placed there, with a piece of thick plastic inside it. The box was filled with the weed, another piece of wood cut to fit went inside the box on top of the weed and a thirty ton hydraulic jack applied pressure until the package was the desired thickness. It did minimal damage to the product. Mostly, the aim was to remove excess air pockets, kind of like vacuum packing food before you freeze it.

Once it was built I transported it across the border and delivered it to Guadalajara. If any Mexican cop had recognized it for what it was I would have spent five years in a Mexican prison just for being in possession of it.

Ah, the lure of danger.

***

Skip forward a bit and let me set the scene. I was with Flaco in a large hacienda on a lake, about an hour's drive from Guadalajara. A pile of burlap bags lay in front of us, about one and a half feet across and four feet high. Each one weighed about fifty pounds and was plump, filled to capacity with weed. These bags were too large and the wrong shape to put into a box container. Most smuggling operations wanted rectangular shapes as they were more efficient. You can fit more weight into the box with compressed rectangles.

Another reason we repackaged was that when buying in bulk in the mountains, the mostly Indian workers and growers inserted large pockets of seeds into the burlap bags. In this way they got rid of superfluous seeds and it padded the bags – and their bottom line. It was a widely recognized practice, expected and included in our bid. Our method of dealing with them when repackaging was to pour the seeds into separate containers and set them aside, not exactly a long term solution.

Eventually, after a year of packing, our separate containers had grown to a full sized pick-up truck bed filled to almost overflowing with seeds. It weighed around a ton. It was a sizable problem in two ways – how to get rid of it, and it was big and impossible to hide. If we were busted while in possession of these seeds our sentences would have been very long.

The distance to Guadalajara from the hacienda was about fifty miles on a two lane black top road. It was not a busy thoroughfare by anyone's standards.

After work one day we were having a few beers and I made a suggestion regarding our seed problem. Flaco was the boss in this operation and had the final say on anything concerning our work.

My suggestion was simple, brilliant really. We buy two large shovels and drive slowly towards Guadalajara while shoveling the seeds into the ditches on either side of the road. He laughed, loving the idea but cautioned that we couldn't start shoveling until we had traveled five or ten miles from the house.

We waited for wet weather, and a little fog to reduce visibility. Then, with a small supply of necessities – beer – we started our drive. We threw shovel full after shovel full on both sides of the road simultaneously, traveling at five to ten miles an hour, laughing and joking the entire time. It took roughly two hours and they were two of the most fun hours I have ever spent.

Problem solved, we put it to the back of our minds and went about our business. Some time later, just after the rainy season, the growing season was in full bloom. Those ditches came alive with a hedge of marijuana. I think almost all the several million seeds came up and flourished. They were two to three feet tall before the army was told to eradicate them. They were out in force for several weeks, pulling each and every plant up one by one. Flaco and I wore permanent huge grins for several months.

As a side note, this proves how easy it is to grow marijuana, and how quickly it is ready for harvest for the multitude of uses this versatile plant offers.

Chapter Three

Medical marijuana relieves pain, suppresses nausea and reduces anxiety

Unexpected problems with the Communist Party of Mexico

This one is a cautionary tale. It is easy, in my line of business, to grow used to the danger, and to become careless. You must stay under the radar, live a quiet life, not be seen in public much, be something of a ghost. In a lot of ways it is a solitary life. The way to be successful, stay successful, and stay alive is to always remember this and not grow complacent. There is little of the romance depicted in movies and television series to this life, and anyone who thinks there is will be destined to learn the hard way.

***

The main boss was another gringo from the valley of Texas. He had lived in Guadalajara for several years and moved many tons of product to the States. He was possibly the richest marijuana mover in Guadalajara. He was not as careful as you might think, or as he should have been. He drove around in a large chauffeur driven Cadillac with bodyguards. This, naturally, made him highly visible and aroused the curiosity and interest of the Communist Party. They were looking for financing for whatever projects they had in the works and sometimes kidnapped people towards this goal. They did not require willing participation.

The boss remained oblivious, despite being warned at least once by his paid off officials before the confrontation. He had become complacent because he bribed the cops and all federal officers. That gave him a false sense of security. I guess, in his defence, it would be unexpected to encounter problems with a political party.

The Communists followed him and mapped out his routes and routines, and he was easy to map because he didn't change either very often. They successfully kidnapped him with little trouble. The ransom they demanded was twenty thousand dollars. This was much less than you may expect. They were paid and let him go as promised. A simple transaction.

At this point, if he had centered himself, thought long and hard about how lucky he was to get out for only twenty thousand, and let it go he may have been okay. But he didn't. He was outraged and paid bribes to find one of their leaders. His ego took control and it was running his show more and more over the next few days. This is never a good idea in any situation. In one such as his, it's a supremely bad idea and that's an understatement.

The boss located one of their leaders and had him beaten severely, although luckily for the boss he did not die. This was a poor reaction since the boss was not harmed at all during his capture and it infuriated the Communist Party.

He reclaimed nine of his twenty thousand and became embroiled in a full-fledged war with the Communist Party – actions have reactions.

This move was just plain stupid, there's no other way to describe it. He was riding around with the carload of bodyguards plus a medium sized truck full of additional bodyguards. This dog and pony show attracted attention from all the worst people.

Our boss kept to his usual routines and patterns, making no effort to make the necessary adjustments demanded by this kind of situation. This was thoughtless and unbelievably foolish.

His car was ambushed. Had there not been added bullet proof glass and armor he would most certainly have been killed. The car was thoroughly, meticulously machine gunned. Finally, he realized he was not the big badass he imagined himself to be.

In a move reminiscent of closing the stable door after the horse has bolted he decided to leave town and move closer to Mexico City. He chose Cuernavaca as his new residence. Another mistake. He thought if he left Guadalajara and surrounded himself with real professionals he would be protected. Bizarrely, he did not understand that the Communist Party was everywhere, especially in Mexico.

The story I heard was that he was in a Volkswagen Beetle, by himself, on the way to Mexico City to buy a Porsche.

Somehow, the Communists managed to follow him and while climbing the mountain between Cuernavaca and Mexico City he was chased off the road. He crashed the Volkswagen and ran into a field where the Communists chased him down, shooting him many times.

This is a horrible story and I was not present at any time for any of it. It is all second hand information but our boss was never seen again. Therefore, I tend to believe most of it.

False modesty is dangerous in my line of work, but so, too, is an over inflated ego.

Chapter Four

Marijuana use eases the pain of Multiple Sclerosis and Fibromyalgia

My Training Progresses

Until the mid 1970's Mexico had a monopoly on the marijuana consumed in America. While most of the drug was transported in cars and trucks, a small percentage was carried by air, and that was where my expertise lay. I was a trained commercial pilot and made many crossings by airplane. However, I needed to learn my chosen profession, and like any business, the only way to do that was from the ground up, so to speak. I got hands on experience in every position and in all the different methods used in smuggling marijuana, but because of my flying skills I began with the aircraft method.

I was working for a man called Paco, who did not usually get himself, his body at least, directly involved. This particular time was different and he was beside me, teaching me the correct way to load an aircraft and all the do's and don'ts of an air short (a short is my slang for an operation that is active and in progress).

Paco gave me a list of the most important aspects of the operation entrusted to the ground crew, stressing all steps must be followed or the aircraft may not make the round trip. Fuel was vital, and we had to top off each tank and ensure the caps were replaced tightly. If a cap was lost all fuel in that tank would siphon out by air pressure caused by the speed of the aircraft. If that happened the aircraft would not have the range needed for the return. It was also important to ensure the load was at its heaviest at the front so it did not interfere with the aircraft's center of gravity.

This was my first experience loading a marijuana smuggling aircraft flown by someone else and I was nervous and apprehensive. I was worried about the unknown aspects of the venture, and afraid I would make a mistake that would jeopardize the outcome and possibly harm the pilot. I needed more experience to become comfortable with this aspect of the job.

Obviously, we could not take off legally from a recognized airport when smuggling, so remote areas with suitable topography were used. On this occasion we were on a dry lake bed in central Mexico, about two hours from Guadalajara. There were many of those, mostly in arid areas. They were easy to spot, a dirty white in color. They did have some water just under the surface so it was important to ensure the aircraft did not go onto those areas.

The way to see them was to look for a gray color and carefully drive the vehicle around the perimeter, marking it with tire treads. Even a light aircraft would sink if it taxied into a moist area and if that happened both the aircraft and the landing spot would be lost.

Paco and I arrived at the lake before the scheduled time and did the setup. We placed a twenty foot pole with a long streamer attached in the ground, and by using a compass found the wind direction. We had to be sure the aircraft landed and took off into the wind. We marked a two thousand foot strip free of obstruction and watery areas.

The smuggling aircraft arrived on time, a small Cessna twin engine. It's a good aircraft for small payloads as it has limited capacity, but has one problem. It will not fly on one engine.

The landing was uneventful and we began with refueling. The return fuel was packaged in fifteen gallon plastic containers with a special attachment device to seal the container to the aircraft fuel intake. I attached the container, rotated it upside down and stabbed holes in its bottom with a thick bladed knife to allow the fuel to flow in the tank as quickly as possible.

Once that was done we loaded the marijuana, and after the last package was in place covered the weed with a cargo net to keep it from shifting in flight, or if a crash happened. If the cargo shifted the pilot ran the risk of being trapped.

Fuelling and loading was done swiftly. The take off area had no obstructions and everything looked to be set for a smooth trip.

Always expect the unexpected.

Remember, this is an aircraft that needs both engines or it can't fly, so when something went majorly wrong with one of the engines on take off it was a disaster. It blew one of the cylinders and lost power, crashing only two miles from where the ground crew was located and still on the edge of the dry lake, fortunately.

We jumped into my truck and raced to the crash site. We had no trouble finding it as a large explosion marked the spot well. Speed was of the essence as a heavy smoke plume indicated fire.

When the plane went down it passed under a tree that tore open the top of the fuselage, providing an escape route for the pilot. We could see him, running slowly from the crash site. He was clearly shocked and confused, and on fire.

To add to the drama, a short time after the crash, with the pilot on fire and heading in a shambling run from the site, the airplane exploded. There were flames leaping into the sky from the plane and the pilot was still running, looking for all the world like a human sized kitchen match.

I was about half the age of Paco so was the first out of the car and the first to reach the pilot. I crash-tackled him, rolling him on the dirt to put out the flames but by this stage he was badly burned.

We were about two hours from medical help.

The pilot was in shock, lying in the back of the truck and hopefully not feeling the vibration from the rough road conditions. Paco and I were on the verge of milder shock. This was not the way it was supposed to go and we were not prepared in any way for such a disaster.

There was silence in the cab, a silence so thick I could taste it.

We had to cope with the many potholes and traffic, mostly eighteen wheeler and buses, that slowed our progress. Three quarter ton pickups such as the one I was driving are notorious for being rough to ride in. Paco was in the back with the pilot and I was driving far faster than should have been possible on that road.

We were racing for Guadalajara, trying to make a plan of action that would not result in the pilot going to jail but would address his wounds as soon as possible. This was the early seventies, no cell phones, no internet, no way of contacting anyone. All we could do was drive as fast as we could to the nearest source of help.

We were fortunate in that we had friends going to medical school in Guadalajara. We went there first but his wounds were too extensive to be treated by our student friends. They called their professors who were wonderfully helpful, saved the pilot's life (I am sure) and did not inform any officials.

The situation was as bad for the pilot as it could be, and still be alive. The doctor said that had we taken as little as an hour or two more to reach help he would most likely have died. Paco and I had his life and his freedom in our hands, a sobering and oppressive feeling. We discussed the few alternatives we had.

The pilot, sensibly, did not want to be turned over to the Mexican officials/cops. He was badly injured but his mind was functioning just fine.

I made a call to the States to another friend, a pilot, to ask a major favor. He agreed to make a rescue flight but had limited range in the only available aircraft. That meant it was necessary to transport the critically ill pilot for nearly ten hours in the back of my truck. It did have a half shell camper on it but the road conditions were poor.

Paco and I conferred with the doctor who said that after a couple of days of treatment we could take the chance and transport him, with great care and attention, and absolutely no guarantee of success. The pilot was informed and had the final say. He made the decision to continue – really, he had little choice. We were apprehensive and worried, feeling the weight of our responsibility for this man.

We agreed on a meeting place and time with the other pilot, another dry lake bed in northern Mexico.

As seemed to be the pattern for this entire debacle, when we arrived at close to the appointed time we found the dry lake was wet, covered by a foot of water. The other pilot was on time, we could see him over the lake. He buzzed us, wagging his wings. We got out of the truck and waved back – we had no means of direct communication.

There was only one road in the area, a two lane black top. We turned on it towards Monterey. You can imagine our state of confusion and worry by this stage. I drove fifty miles without seeing much of anything in that sparsely populated desert region.

In Mexico there is a gas station chain named Pemex. Out here, in the middle of nowhere, there was a lone station. As we passed it we noticed the aircraft parked in the Pemex, like it had pulled up so the driver could get a cup of coffee. We pulled in and transferred our wounded man into the aircraft. One of the Pemex workers, unfazed, jumped into a vehicle and blocked the road close to the Pemex in one direction while I went half a mile the other way. The rescue pilot took off in the stretch of road between us. It sounds like the finale to a movie, but it was real life.

***

The end of this story is, under the circumstances, a good one.

The injured pilot ended up in a burn unit in San Antonio, Texas, recovering well. He watched his own story on television, a story about a week old by that stage. The footage showed a melted airplane with nothing discernible except the engine. The aircraft was incinerated, no evidence left for the investigating team to ever fully understand what the plane was doing on a lake bed.

The burn victim retired from smuggling.

There were no repercussions from our backers. I was always straight up and honest. I told the truth and expected truth in return and backers trusted me. My word was never proved wrong. And there was no load left, none, so no investigation of any kind ever came out of that misadventure.

And me? After that experience I flew with two 357 magnum pistols in shoulder holsters. They were not for protection, but to ensure I never burned. The idea was that after the crash I would have been able to find at least one of the pistols.

When you live on the edge of danger you have to expect that at any time it might turn that edge and cut you. It's how you deal with it when it happens that makes the difference.

Chapter Five

Marijuana treats inflammatory bowel disease by making the intestinal cells bond tightly together

Jamaica - the free Mexican airforce is off course!

While on the subject of smuggling with aircraft, I will tell you another tale, one of my more foolish trips. For this trip I did something out of character and learned a valuable lesson from it. I have always preferred to be in control of everything because when you rely on other people you are leaving yourself open to their potential mistakes, forgetfulness, or lack of care. But for this trip, I hired myself out for a fee. Read on to see how that turned out.

It was a variation on my usual style in more ways than just one. I had a crop dusting friend who owned a private strip in southern central Louisiana and he offered me the use of it. I was only too happy to use a secure landing spot like that but there was a small problem – isn't there always? This trip, as I said, was a bit different, and my destination was Jamaica, fourteen hundred miles each way.

The flight would take at least eighteen hours, and had to be completed within a twenty-four hour window. Cuba was forcing any small aircraft down that ventured into their airspace. So the flight had to be a longer one, over the waters of the Caribbean and the Gulf of Mexico, in a single engine airplane that was feeling flimsier each time I thought about the practicalities. The range of the aircraft was one thousand nautical miles and I needed twice that – at a minimum. A reserve was imperative in case of errors, issues, delays etc. I allowed myself a five hundred mile cushion which would have been sufficient for a normal trip. I don't know why I classified this as a normal trip.

At that time the government made it so difficult to get current weather projections that it could be considered impossible. The only way was to file a flight plan, which, of course, was not possible. People like me had to become good at predicting the weather which was another impossibility given the lack of equipment and the distances involved.

Bearing all this in mind, I placed a bladder of fuel in the fuselage which took up a third of the space available for the load. I explained what I had done and why to my employers, ensuring we were all on the same page and they understood the load capacity of the aircraft was cut in half. Remember this point for later. They knew the load capacity was halved.

There was a cold front passing and I waited two days for the winds to calm. This was my only personal mistake on this trip, other than agreeing to it in the first place. Remember what I said about lack of equipment and distance making it impossible to judge the weather? It meant a lot of assumptions had to be made.

I took off at two in the morning, on a night with no moon, flying without navigational aids over the Gulf of Mexico. My first indication of trouble was when I reached Cancun two hours early – I had a forty knot tail wind. I almost missed seeing Cancun due to the cloud cover. Off to a great start.

I am not such a bull headed person that I did not have qualms. I did and I should have turned back. My sixth sense was clamoring for me to turn back but I didn't as my sense of responsibility was stronger. People were waiting for me and depending on me and I have always followed through on my commitments. I continued, turning left on a heading for the Caymans, thinking the wind would abate – like I could predict the weather. The winds held steady, gusts all the way.

In the late seventies, Jamaica was well aware of the popularity of their marijuana, especially the people who lived close to the few airstrips available to people like me. Everyone must be paid and that included those people.

On landing, an aircraft would be surrounded by about two hundred people expecting a five thousand dollar tip. Of course, there was no official need to pay. All that would happen if you chose not to pay would be large rocks rolled onto the strip, placed to ensure you could not take off. The rocks would be, naturally, larger than you and your small ground crew would be able to successfully remove. I believe you could call this 'passive aggressive' behavior.

On this night, I arrived to find my ground crew waiting along with the locals. Normally I carry enough fuel with me for the round trip, but this flight was so long I couldn't carry a double load as the extra weight would have made it impossible to take off. I had to trust the ground crew in Jamaica had brought real aviation fuel and not car gas.

I was relieved to see the fuel was aviation fuel, one potential problem I could stop worrying about. I fuelled first and positioned the load on top of the bladder – my extended range extra fuel tank. This was when I discovered the load had been trash compacted. I had limited weight I could carry and I was concerned about the weight of this load. I asked questions, lots of questions, and was assured it was not more than four hundred pounds in weight. I made the reluctant decision to proceed. I really should have listened to my inner voice that has never led me wrong.

Remember the locals waiting for their tip? The method of payment is rather crude as the time for something fairer was never available. The cash brought for the tip was always small denominations, fives, tens, and twenties. The payment method was like something you would see in a movie about smuggling – but it was how it was really done. Two to four handfuls of cash was thrown as high as possible into the air, allowing the wind to disperse it.

Of course, the biggest, strongest, and most aggressive of the people waiting who were of all ages, shapes, and health, got most of it. That's a pretty good metaphor for life.

I studied the runway. I had roughly three thousand feet of less than smooth runway with obstructions at the end. Fifty foot obstructions, in the shape of a coconut plantation.

My inner voice screaming at me I pushed the plane back as far as possible to utilize every inch of that three thousand feet. As the run for take off started the engine began to labor, but once started there was no stopping. The brakes were not designed for this much weight and I would have plowed into the plantation. I firewalled the throttle – opened it to the fullest – and crossed my fingers.

Those fifty foot palm trees are mighty big up close when you are still on the ground and not soaring above them. I kept a hard forward pressure on the yoke and waited until it was a choice between crash it or make it, unable to push out of my mind the knowledge that there was twice the fuel which would make any crash explosive. The poor pilot of the previous chapter was in my mind. I did not want to live through his experience and had the gun to ensure it would not happen.

Right at the base of the palm trees, at the absolute last second, I pulled back on the yoke. The plane lurched into the air, just missing the top of the trees. The stall horn was blowing, an ear piercing sound. A stall horn is a reed similar to that used in a musical instrument, mounted on one wing. It plays when the plane is at an angle that will cause a stall. I had never heard that horn blow as loud as it did on this take off.

My airspeed was so slow I should not have been able to fly. I was balanced on a knife edge, not gaining or losing speed, suspended less than fifty feet above those palm trees. Instead of lifting gracefully I was plowing the air, somehow not falling out of the sky. As much as a hair's width of a change to the yoke and you would not now be reading this story. I would be a statistic, unrecorded. I would have disappeared from the earth.

I maintained that altitude for thirty heart stopping miles before the airspeed indicator began to rise, slowly. The Caymans were a hundred and fifty miles away and by the time I got there I had climbed less than two thousand feet. To this day I am firmly convinced my sphincter pulled that aircraft up! My employers had grossly overloaded me which put me at extreme peril. There were angry words in their near future.

On the return trip the forty knot tailwind had become a headwind, and possibly stronger. There was no way I could make Louisana without going over Cuba and even then it would be close. There was cloud cover at seven thousand feet and the only plan I had was to fly through that fluffy camouflage and hope they did not want to spend the fuel to intercept me. My luck held, and the Cubans did not come to greet me.

Over the open water I was constantly scanning the horizon for ships. I was acutely aware of the extreme strain on the engine, not to mention the extreme strain on my nerves. If it became too much and the engine quit I planned to land near a ship and, hopefully, be seen and rescued.

My method for returning to the States from a gulf crossing was simple. The average speed of a helicopter is one hundred and twenty knots. I would drop down to one thousand feet and back off the airspeed to just below this rate. The gulf was full of petroleum helicopters. I did my best to blend in, hiding in plain sight.

My anxiety level rose in direct correlation with the way the fuel gauges were dropping. Only one fuel gauge showed fuel available and it had a whisker showing, less than a width of a fuel indicator. There were still seventy-five to a hundred nautical miles to go.

Finally, anxiety levels off the charts and my heart in my mouth, I landed at my friend's strip. I have never been more pleased to complete a trip. I checked the tanks to see how much fuel was left. Out of five tanks, four were dry and the last had less than half an inch, maybe ten or fifteen minutes flight.

I had taken off in a plane so overloaded it should have crashed back there at the coconut trees. I had made it through Cuban airspace, battled a strong headwind, used up all but a drop of fuel and landed safely. Truly, I was blessed with abundant good fortune!

I could add more to this story but that would be to add some more complaints and making threats to the bastards who had such little regard for my life. I vowed never to work for them, or anyone else, again. People who do not get their bodies directly involved and have no thought for the safety of those who do are despicable and cowardly.

The only person you can rely on is yourself.

Chapter Six

Marijuana relieves the pain and discomfort of rheumatoid arthritis and promotes sleep

CIA/Colombian Trip

This is another of those 'what was I thinking?' stories. I became involved in this one late, called in to solve problems in a trip that was screwed up. Why ask me? Because I was damn good at what I did. Why did I do it? I don't know – when a trip is screwed up it almost never rights itself. Maybe that was why, right there. Maybe, as an adrenalin junkie, I did it because I knew it might get dangerous. Perhaps I allowed my ego to swell a little, thinking I was the only one who could fix this mess.

By the time I entered the picture there was a boat circling in the Gulf of Mexico with twenty-six tons on board and a compromised offload. The plan had been to offload in a small town of around five thousand people on the West coast of Florida, but the Federal and State cops had locked down the town and no-one was allowed in or out of the harbor without Government permission. Obviously, there was no chance of getting Government permission.

In that small town most everyone was involved in offloading, performing a service but not getting involved any further in the business. It was a case of proximity – since they lived there they may as well take advantage of easy money.

I signed on to assist with a possible offload of the marijuana and also to provide a stash house. At that late stage I was unable to put the offload together fast enough to have made a difference so switched my focus to the stash house.

Here's a rule to remember, the reason for which you will learn if you keep on reading: Never, ever, immediately use a strange new rental. Wait at least three months for any carry-over problems from the previous tenant to show up (literally).

The first clear indication that I should not have accepted this job came when I was introduced to a room full of Cubans. This disturbed me greatly. There was a huge gray area in this business, one everyone knew about and few talked about. Certain people were involved in this lucrative business for their own reasons and I preferred, in fact made it a personal rule, to never work directly with them. Who am I talking about? Let's just call them the alphabets, and I knew which alphabet agency hired these Cubans, historically, and I was anxious. My antennae, my built in warning signal that never led me wrong (except when I willfully ignored it) was bristling but by this stage I was too involved to walk away without repercussions.

Since I was the only person who knew the location of the stash house it was necessary for me to go to the exchange from the offload over to the Cubans, which was to be in Baton Rouge, Louisiana.

Several Jartran trucks arrived, driven by people wearing the United States customs uniforms. This, understandably as I am sure you would agree, made me very nervous and confirmed my suspicions.

With no choice but to continue we took the trucks to the house and unloaded the goods. It was a medium small house and barely held the volume of product. Fortunately –

well not fortunately, deliberately – it was in a rural area of Louisiana with few neighboring homes and none in sight.

We finished and were taking a breather, me beginning to relax for the first time since I realized who we were dealing with, when a lone police car pulled into the driveway and stopped at the gate.

Before this single police car appeared nobody was armed. The car pulled up, and instantly the Cubans had Uzis. Where they got them from I don't know, but it was chilling how swiftly they appeared. In contrast, my friend, who rented the house, and I were unarmed. And feeling pretty naked I must say.

The Cubans wanted to solve the problem by shooting the policeman – who was on his own – and leave. They had no investment and were hired only to do their part of the offload. I managed to stop them, told them to chill, and went to talk to the policeman. My friend and I went out and discovered he was nothing more than a process server looking for the former occupant. When I explained we were just moving in and did not know the former tenant he was not even a little bit curious.

I think about him sometimes - the poor guy never knew how close he came to checking out that day.

And that, folks, is why you never use a new rental house right away.

***

There were two friends involved with this trip, let's call them Numb Nuts and John.

The first one talked me into the job – Numb Nuts. He had to know more about it than he disclosed to me. This made me very unhappy with him, and that is an understatement. He was the go-between for any contact with the silent, invisible owners.

The second, John, was in charge of sales. He, like me, did not know this was a Government job. On being informed he decided to keep working. I was, out of necessity, sitting on the sidelines. The only reason I was still around was to be ready to leave the country if it became necessary. The only way I could know that was to stick around so there I was.

The Cubans went home to little Miami and did not much else on this short, including receiving payments. John was left with the problem.

John was there because he, too, was very good at his job. In the first three weeks he dispatched one to two thousand pounds of product a day, all of it up front with little down stroke. That was the way almost all sales on larger trips were conducted. You looked the man in the eye and shook his hand. That was your contract and your word was your bond. There is a term most people are familiar with, honor among thieves, and in those days it was true. Nowadays it's a different story, sadly.

Little money returned in those first three weeks, but then around a half million or a million came in daily. That's a lot of money in anyone's language.

I was impressed at how well John had his business together and began to think it would all work out.

The money owed was considerable and the pile grew daily. Numb Nuts, the go-between, could not get the Cubans to come and pick up the money. Whoever the handlers/owners were, they did not show their faces.

Then Numb Nuts' father died and he had to go to the funeral. This was not his fault of course, and sad for him, but we were left with a large sum of money. Who should you trust with around ten million of other people's money? On the practical side, the sheer volume and mass of such an amount is staggering – and you'd be staggering trying to carry it. It was eighteen medium sized suitcases full, with lots of twenties. There's a visual for you. Eighteen suitcases full of cash.

I sat for a week in an expensive hotel room with excellent security. I got to know every maid and room service person well. It was not fun, by any stretch of the imagination.

Numb Nuts finally returned and I was happy to see him and be free of my confinement. I handed the room over to him and left.

Somehow the people owed the money finally showed up, everybody was paid and the trip ended successfully.

I vowed to never get involved with a troubled trip again.

As far as I was aware there was no CIA involved in this one, but it doesn't do to dig too deeply in those gray areas.

***

While on the subject of offloads, here's another story, this one a successful Colombian offload with the addition of bribed cops.

We had police protection in a small Gulf of Mexico coastal town. The offload was on an old and in the main deserted dock. The boat was close and we had arrived with two eighteen wheelers and an old school bus. One eighteen was empty, and the other contained gravity skate wheel conveyors and scaffolding. The bus was for our offload crew, about twenty people.

It took about two hours to set up the scaffolding and rollers, before bringing the boat in and beginning the offload. The distance was the length of a football field, boat to truck. The idea behind the scaffold and rollers was speed, giving us the ability to unload many tons in a short space of time.

The cops were in a fan-shaped perimeter about a quarter of a mile out.

It took us longer to get the product up and out of the stash on the boat than it did to transport it to the empty eighteen wheeler on the rollers. We emptied the boat and filled the eighteen wheeler which drove away as soon as all the packages were loaded.

We broke down the rollers and scaffolding and left, by which time the product had been gone for two hours.

I'm telling this story because this is the best and least risky offload I saw. It was the creation of an old friend who did not have any problems as far as I knew.

Credit where credit is due, hats off to that friend!

Chapter Seven

Marijuana improves the metabolism and promotes a healthier response to sugar in the body

Kindness and Marketing

Act of Random Kindness

As I have said before, I was born lucky. That and my sixth sense saved me from sticky situations many times. This time it was my luck, or guardian angel, whichever you like to call it.

I was in far South Oaxaca, Mexico, driving a Ford three quarter ton pick-up truck on a high and curvy road. Now saying it had curves is a bit like saying Marilyn Monroe had curves. This road had killer curves. It was a two lane, no dividing strip mountain road. There were no railings to halt a plummet over the side, and no curve markers of any kind. It was a switchback road, tight left, then right, one after the other, for a hundred miles. In dry conditions it was challenging, in rain impossible. Top speed was thirty miles an hour or less in good conditions. Of course, it was raining.

Negotiating a curve I hit a slick spot, did a one-eighty and swapped ends, then went over the edge. Fortunately, the truck I was driving had a large muffler that hung low. As the front wheels went slowly over the edge the muffler dug in and stopped the truck, without a tire touching the ground.

I sat in the driver seat, shocked, but feeling lucky.

The truck was teetering on the edge of the cliff. I edged the door open and slid out. Holding onto the truck I crept as carefully as I could hand over hand back to the tailgate where I sat.

Now I was in a quandary. If I got up I would lose the truck. I couldn't even leave it long enough to gather rocks for a counter balance, or get any possessions out of the cab.

Feeling foolish and thoroughly screwed, I resigned myself to losing the truck due to my impatience. Should have gone slower. The road had little traffic. I sat for an hour and not one vehicle passed.

Then, before I decided to give up and stand up, an old third class bus came around the corner. I didn't even wave at the driver but I guess my situation spoke for itself. The bus driver stopped and jumped out, moved to the back of the bus and got out his chains. His half a bus load of passengers did not say a single negative word.

Can you imagine that reaction in the States? Nah, the driver wouldn't even have stopped and the passengers would have been too busy filming me in my hopeless situation to care.

Back to the story. The driver attached the chains and swiftly saved my ass. He didn't say one word. He was of Indian heritage and probably did not speak much Spanish. He unhooked the chains and returned them to their storage before jumping back behind the wheel ready to leave. I stood next to him, trying to give him nearly all the money I had.

This man just saved a total stranger thousands, and expected nothing for it, not even thanks.

I stuffed the money in his shirt pocket and got off the bus. If I didn't hurry I would be going wherever the bus was going.

There was a time when our society used to be like that, helping someone without thinking of a possible reward but just out of humanity. I hope we can return to that mindset. The world would definitely be a better place. In my time I saw a lot of human kindness from the Mexicans, a truly wonderful people. In the early days there was a code of honor among smugglers as well, but times change and nothing stays the same.

But no matter what else happens, an act of random kindness will always send ever expanding ripples out into the universe and if there is enough kindness it will change the whole world. I believe this wholeheartedly.

***

The following are two quick stories about marketing.

Marketing in San Francisco

I was in San Francisco in 1978. I had arrived in town with fifteen hundred pounds of very fine Mexican.

My problem was that they had just begun spraying defoliants and Mexican was not wanted, especially in California. The customers were totally ignorant and did not know what to expect. My load was clean, as were most products out of Mexico, but any fear tactic is always effective in the United States.

I sat in a Ho-Jo's in Marin Co. for over a month – that's a Howard Johnsons. I had investors and partners to answer to. It made it imperative the sale was completed in a timely fashion but my expense budget was blown. Nobody was buying.

To fix this problem I smuggled the load to Hawaii, and sold it back to mostly the same people in San Francisco, as low-grade Hawaiian, charging a little more for the extra expense. Sometimes it just takes a little imagination.

Marketing in New York

I had a crossing on a lake in Texas on the Rio Grande. I'd purchased around two tons of excellent green and red Mexican pot and planned on taking it to New York. I knew just any weed would not work in New York. They were picky and enjoyed the fact that they were the largest and hardest to satisfy market in the United States.

I crossed the weed and took it to Austin, Texas and set up a good smuggling system for the States. It would look like a heavy duty pick-up truck pulling a large trailer full of scaffolding and scaffolding boards. The offload and stash house was to be in Pennsylvania. I planned to take it to New York in smaller increments as needed.

I arrived without incident and transferred a large sample to my salespeople in the city. They shopped it for several days and informed me that nobody was interested. This puzzled me, because I had never been totally turned down as my product was always upscale and looked and worked very well.

I got feedback from three or four long term friends who did not know each other, all saying the same things about my product. It was very good BUT everyone in the city was asking for brown pot, like Colombian. It was 1980 and the Colombian pot tidal wave had struck. Brown pot was in vogue everywhere in the city. All the best people were smoking it exclusively, tongue in cheek. The pot business was strange, especially on the sales end, and it did not get any stranger than New York. I had brought several loads there and had many nit-picking issues with locals.

My city stash house was unique, in one of the boroughs slightly outlying the Manhattan area. It was a two story house with a different type of neighbor on the right hand side. A man and his entire family lived there, Italians. At that time the disco craze was in full swing. This man drove a limo for the local Don who ran the mafia family in control of the borough. That made our house extremely secure. No crime of any kind occurred on this block. The cops drove by regularly and never looked in our direction. We could not have been safer.

When our neighbor got off work and returned home to park the limo there were two parked, one behind the other, with our truck parked in front.

He was a sight to see. He would get out dressed in the disco fashions of the day, disco music blaring from his sound system. His nickname from us was Tony Manero, John Travolta's character in Saturday Night Fever.

I did not, and still do not, like disco and that movie in particular. I did appreciate the fact that I was getting protection just by the accident of the house being next door to the Don's limo driver. I have always led a charmed life.

Back to my story. I was stuck with two tons that nobody seemed interested in. I sat for three weeks and still hadn't sold much. I was starting to consider making another drive to a different market in Idaho, of all places. It was two thousand miles away and as different to New York as night and day. Idaho was very slow, and New York very fast.

I had expected to be fully paid in two weeks or less and Idaho would take at least a month or more. I decided to wait a little longer and see if I could come up with a new plan.

I was wandering around the city, going to museums, art galleries, and other interesting places. I wandered into an antique shop, just window shopping, and spotted a stack of newspapers from South America, from Argentina. I had one of those flashes of an idea and bought the newspapers. There were enough of them to put my new plan into motion.

I went back to the stash house and rewrapped the load of marijuana in those newspapers, and renamed it Argentine Green. I called my salespeople and put it out with the new name.

It sold out in less than a week. Trendy people want trendy names.

One of those talents that can't be taught is how to think outside the box

Chapter Eight

Marijuana releases dopamine, and spurs creativity

Escape Acapulco

The free Mexican air force hits a bump.

> "The Nixon campaign in 1968, and the Nixon White House after that, had two enemies: the antiwar left and black people. You understand what I'm saying? We knew we couldn't make it illegal to be either against the war or blacks, but by getting the public to associate the hippies with marijuana and blacks with heroin, and then criminalizing both heavily, we could disrupt those communities. We could arrest their leaders, raid their homes, break up their meetings, and vilify them night after night on the evening news. Did we know we were lying about the drugs? Of course we did."
> John Ehrlichman, to Dan Baum for Harper's Magazine in 1994, about President Richard Nixon's war on drugs, declared in 1971.[1]

I was on a bus halfway between San Antonio and Austin, Texas, on Interstate 35, about to make a scheduled stop in San

---

[1] Dan Baum. "Legalize it all, How to win the war on drugs", Harper's Magazine, August 8th, 2017,
https://harpers.org/archive/2016/04/legalize-it-all/

Marcos. Home was thirty miles away. The bus was an older one, with a short flight of stairs and two restrooms across from each other in the middle of the vehicle.

The only passengers were me and the bus driver, and up the stairs eight or nine Mexican men who were doing their best to act like they were not traveling together. I was not fooled.

I was sitting, trying to stay calm, behind the driver so I could check the large rear view mirror aimed at the interior of the bus. From the exit it was less than four minutes' drive to the bus station. As soon as we took the exit all the Mexicans stood up at once and began a fast advance to the front. I was expecting this and was faster than them, jumping into one of the restrooms and locking the door.

They beat and kicked the restroom door for several minutes but it was old and built well so they had no luck. I guess they forgot to bring a crowbar. For his own reasons, the driver failed to report this behavior in San Marcos. The stop was short, and the bus continued the journey to Austin. I stayed in the restroom until the bus was back up to highway speeds on the interstate.

When I finally opened the door I saw the Mexicans were still on the bus, but had moved and were sitting around my erstwhile seat and the driver. I waited until we were four or five blocks from the Austin bus station before I spoke to the driver for the first time. He was, understandably, nervous and clearly disturbed. I was, too. I asked a favor.

***

To understand how I got into this predicament we have to go back to the beginning of the story. At this stage of my career I was still naïve, not understanding the political aspect to being a drug smuggler, or the way it could impact on my life. This was a hard lesson to learn and there were times I thought I would never escape from it. Smuggling was not as straightforward as it may appear. Politics added unexpected, unpredictable and ever more dangerous edges to my life, and the lives of everyone involved in this game.

***

Just after Christmas, 1973, a young couple from Texas, with infant daughter on board, left on a driving trip to Acapulco, Mexico. The trip had the dual purpose of business and pleasure. The plan was to spend New Year's in Acapulco and explore a job offer for the husband. If the job was accepted the mother and daughter would fly home.

At that time I occasionally took my young family along with me, something I finally realized was far too dangerous. But not at that point.

***

I began negotiations with someone I knew little about and did not trust. He was the kind of person who did not risk himself but hired others to take the risk. The people in this category were few and usually inept and cowardly, and did not pay sufficient attention to detail since it was not their bodies on the line. Basically, they were nothing more than bankers.

I needed investment money to fly an air short out of Mexico. I had all the equipment necessary but lacked the cash to buy the product. Because of this my focus was in the wrong spot and I made a mistake.

I had just driven the route that would be used to return to the States. There were no checks on the road, which would not last, so it was necessary to make the jump to the border as soon as possible.

The banker assured me everything was in order. The most dangerous portion of the trip was from Acapulco to Zihuatanejo and back. At that time no road north of Zwhat existed. If you wanted to visit you had to travel to Acapulco and drive west. It was only one hundred and twenty kilometers but during those years that particular stretch of highway was the most dangerous on the planet. Only six weeks earlier I had declined a job moving a much larger load down that same road.

The banker swore he had the trip paid off, and police would ride along with us acting as though they had busted us and we were being transported to Acapulco for charges. I did not like working for cops, and still don't. They disgust me, but sometimes they are a necessary evil. The banker swore, over and over, that everything was organized.

I cannot say why I said yes. I have no valid excuse. My antenna was going off, and it has never led me wrong. I just hadn't learned to listen. This time it didn't seem to be loud enough for me to say no. In retrospect, it probably was but I was so focused on how I needed the investment money I didn't listen. I was going to earn four thousand dollars for this trip which was enough to buy what I needed.

The banker made a promise to drive the point car and assist with coordination, which was the deciding factor, so I said yes. We had poor quality CB radios with a short range of only three miles. That meant we needed to stay close together and that made us more vulnerable.

Rich was the main driver and he was all for it. I was there to back up and if necessary put any weed that did not fit in his vehicle into mine. We were out on a limb, and that shit banker was about to saw it off. But I said yes, and my word was, and is, my bond. Once more that damn banker assured me everything was taken care of.

I made air reservations for my wife and daughter to leave two days later.

Very early the next day Rich and I left as it was important we were back to Acapulco by early evening. The later after dark it was the more danger of a bust there would be. The army and local cops did not usually put up roadblocks until late in the evening so as not to inconvenience the tourists.

During that year they were using the kidnapping of Patty Hearst as an excuse for checks so it was possible one could be on that road at any time.

The road was picturesque, traveling through small towns and in almost constant sight of the Pacific Ocean, with mountains reaching down to the ocean. The view was lovely, verdant green everywhere. There were coconut palm plantations interspersed with mango, papaya and other tropical fruits. It was a lush garden spot. The whole road was raised between five and ten feet. Every year there were at least one if not more severe tropical storms bringing many inches of rain in a short time frame. If the road was not elevated it would have been unusable. Marijuana grew very well there, along with everything else. It was the number one cash crop and everyone who lived in the area profited from the trade, either directly or indirectly.

There was very little cover for our two pick-up trucks with half shell campers, plus one missing point car.

***

We arrived at the meeting area early and, as usual, the cops and the farmers were not there. The banker was also a no show.

The farmers were bringing the load down from the mountains. We did not know that because that lying banker told us it was already in a small house, waiting for us to arrive. If we had known, we would have said no and would not have been there. I wish we had left, instead of waiting for ten hours but you cannot leave people hanging with a load when it has been ordered. That would be inappropriate, to say the least. It could cost them their freedom, or their lives. My word was my bond and I would not go back on it.

That was an unstable time for Guerrero. During those years there were revolutionaries - Lucio Cabanas (the leader of the Party of the Poor) - and others living in the mountains. The people we were waiting for may well have been with them. There was a small scale, undeclared war raging all around us. Everyone in the region was armed and had chosen sides.

I found out that we were an unknown factor. Our boss had not done his homework and misrepresented (lied) about his relationship with the farmers and the police.

There were no hotels or restaurants close enough to the meeting place that would have been feasible for us to hang out in. Our choices were severely limited.

We finally made contact with the farmers but they had difficulty traveling down the trail with an army patrol. Their train was made up of fifteen animals loaded with the weed, plus mules and burros for the people doing the work to ride so they could move faster. That was not easy to hide and everyone living along the trail could see what was happening. Blind Freddy could have seen what was happening.

The Government had many ex-captives living everywhere. They had been tortured and their families threatened with death if they did not provide information when asked. This put almost everyone at odds with each other. They stayed within their family units or with trusted friends and co-workers. The muscle of the army and genuine fear of the government was very real, and palpable.

The trail system they used was extensive and extremely well kept and was the only way the mostly Indian population had to travel for work, buy supplies, or sell the products they manufactured. The things they manufactured ranged from food to hand made carvings, embroidery, pottery and an almost endless list of things. They were prolific and gave back much to the Mexican culture. When the trail became degraded by age or the rainy season all the people living close to the damaged area would get together and make the necessary repairs in a timely fashion. This socialistic system of mutual support impressed me. In my experience this system was far superior to ours, especially when cost was factored in.

The lives those people lived was difficult to say the least but their attitudes were positive and giving.

***

The people we were waiting for were tempered and extremely tough but they were nervous and apprehensive when they arrived.

We moved two kilometers and made the exchange. By that time it was two in the morning, probably the worst time of day to make the run to Acapulco.

The banker and the cops did not show. I found out later that the cops, being drunk, were busted by the army and ratted us out. So, with that bit of information, it would not have mattered when we left because they were waiting.

We had no point car for any warning, our radios were short range and of no real use. We had a choice to make – throw the load away or complete our contract. Rich was broke and determined to complete the contract with or without me.

I counseled Rich to toss it, but he refused to consider it.

I was stuck and could not leave him to the fates, but as it turns out it would not have made a difference unless we threw the load away. We drove the short distance to the paved road. I turned left towards Acapulco and Rich, about a mile behind, for some reason turned the wrong way. I thought he was just nervous and confused. He drove ten, maybe fifteen miles before realizing it was the wrong direction. By then we were thirty miles apart and the radios had no hope of working.

One of the farmers was sitting in the truck with me. He'd asked for a ride to Acapulco and his nonchalance was a factor in my decision to continue.

I travelled another thirty miles, trying the whole time to raise Rich on the radio.

The farmer and I arrived in the largest town between Acapulco and Zwhat. It was around three o'clock in the morning in Tecpan, and it felt like a ghost town. I drove through a series of short turns one or two blocks long in the city center. I could not see ahead because the view was obstructed by one and two story buildings. No one was moving and there was absolutely no traffic. The feeling was kind of like that of being naked in a crowd.

There were two final turns to make, a right and a quick left which put us on a small concrete bridge over a river, and nowhere to run.

At that point I saw something that made me wish I was still lonely. Ranged in front of me were fifty, maybe seventy heavily armed Mexican soldiers.

It was a pitch black night, no moon, almost no lights in the village. My headlights were the brightest things there. The soldiers were using their bodies as a road block. There was no vehicle or barricade in sight. I stopped just short of the group of soldiers. Ten or fifteen, I wasn't sure, were strung up the road, placed where they could shoot into the front of any vehicle trying to run through the check. So that was not a viable option.

A sergeant, the one in charge, approached the driver's side and asked where the brown truck was. I was in a blue one, Rich's was brown. This was the first positive that we had been given up by the banker and his police.

He pulled me out of the truck and demanded that I open the camper. His face fell when he saw it was empty. This made him unsure I was involved and gave him a problem. He didn't know what to do so began by taking my wallet and walking around, with me following, stealing most of my expense money.

By this stage it was between five and ten minutes since my arrival and I could not imagine why Rich hadn't shown up.

They started searching the truck and asking the hitchhiker/farmer what he was doing there. Thirty minutes passed and they ran out of options and had stolen my money so there was no reason for me to be there. All the soldiers up the road were now around the truck, out of position, all weapons cocked and locked.

***

They had just given me my keys when Rich rounded the corner. He was moving pretty fast and had to brake so he did not hit one of them. The only good decision he made was at this point. Instead of a full stop, he gunned it and made several of them dive out of the way, and drove as fast as the truck could go up the road.

The soldiers were momentarily surprised before they all started firing. Night turned to day from the muzzle flashes and the noise was a shock in the still night. The back of the truck was blown up, the left rear tire shot out and the truck veered dangerously, going sideways. It recovered, and continued down the road. Two things saved Rich, the back of the truck being completely full of weed and the soldiers having moved out of their assigned positions. Otherwise he would have been dead.

The soldiers had no transportation. I reacted quickly and tossed my truck keys over the bridge into the water. Fortunately for me, nobody saw me do this.

During the gunplay I had a close call. One of the soldiers standing three feet from my truck pointed his weapon at the side of the truck and motioned with the muzzle of his weapon for me to leave. I didn't have the keys, and if I did and tried to leave both the hitchhiker/farmer and I would have died. For some reason, this soldier wanted to kill a Gringo that morning.

The sergeant pulled me out of the truck and frantically searched for the keys. Not finding them he had me and the hitchhiker searched, along with the truck and surrounding area.

The sergeant was frustrated as he began to realize he had failed his mission. His superiors would be most unhappy with his performance. His next move was to send for a local mechanic. The mechanic hotwired the truck and finally got it started. This all took about an hour. Instead of chasing the brown truck they took me and the farmer to their army base and locked us up.

***

Meanwhile, Rich, after driving through that hail of lead was in the process of hyperventilating. Up until that point he had done an outstanding job.

The truck was hard to handle with the ton of marijuana and the left rear tire shot out. He had driven the rubber off the rim. His highest speed was around thirty miles an hour. He had traveled seven or eight miles and there were no lights from behind or in front of him. So, if he had centered himself and gathered his thoughts both of us would have gotten through the experience – but he didn't.

He was in the process of panicking. Not one vehicle had passed in either direction since well before the problem of the roadblock. The locals did not move after around ten in the evening because it was too dangerous.

Rich decided to abandon the truck, a good decision if he had driven it as far off the road as he could get it and buried it in the dense foliage. The people living along the coast would have taken the load and resold it which would have been a windfall for them. Our problem would have been solved. Not one of the peasants would have had anything to do with the army or police. They feared them for good reason. When interrogated they were tortured.

Rich, instead of hiding the truck, left it in the middle of the road which was a major mistake.

During his headlong flight he lost his glasses. Being blind without them complicated a complicated situation even more. He was rudderless and blind. This is why you should never work with inexperienced people.

At this juncture things had worked out for our crew about as well as it possibly could have. Then Rich's inability to cope screwed both of us.

To save himself all Rich had to do was walk a couple of hundred yards from the road and continue towards Acapulco. It was only around thirty miles. A short walk and he would have been home free.

Meanwhile, at the army post, they finally began searching for the brown truck. With no other vehicle available they piled into my truck and went about ten miles, to find Rich's truck blocking half the road, still loaded with weed.

This was hours after the drama at the checkpoint and the sun had been up for some time. That probably saved the sergeant's stripes so he was happy.

They changed the tire and sent the loaded truck back to Tecpen. The sergeant was down to less than ten men and because there were revolutionaries throughout the region he never went off the road with less than fifty men. It could have been suicide for him to look for the driver so he elected to drive up and down the road looking for his fugitive.

They drove up and down until Rich walked out of the bush right into their hands. One very happy sergeant whose luck wiped out all his mistakes.

Rich was a dumb ass. Amateurs were and are the bane of my life. He did such a good job, then took a dump all over it and me. I had nothing in my truck but I was charged for what was in Rich's truck.

We were taken to Acapulco and charged equally. The hitchhiker/farmer was set free.

Acapulco Jail

I arrived at the jail on the second or third day of January 1974, after being held for a day or two by the army.

The first thing I noticed was the strange layout. In places it looked more like a cheap bar than a jail. Everything was painted hot pink, if you can imagine that. It seemed a large hotel had given the jail hundreds of gallons of the damned stuff and they repainted every two months so it was always vibrantly pink. I grew to hate that color and still do forty years later.

They guided me through the surprisingly few locked and barred doors and delivered Rich and me to the top of a small hill where the tiny guard house was located. It was right next to the window where most of the business with the outside world was conducted for the inmates. The market deliveries and short term visits were also held there.

From there I was taken past the small infirmary, down a short flight of stairs and to a large barred entry gate.

I entered Jail Number 2, Carcel Numero Dose.

It was very small, perhaps the square footage of three basketball courts. One was an actual basketball court and another what we called the chicken coop, with two hundred and fifty concrete bunks stacked three high. Every night at six they held the list and locked up around one thousand people in it. Do the math.

The third court size was taken up by work areas for the mostly tourist based products manufactured by the inmates.

I was logical in my approach to this dilemma. There was no point in collapsing in a heap. I had to survive as comfortably as I could until I could find a way out of this place. I forced my mind to not focus on the type of people in here and the fact that I had no backup or help, and stuck to the practicalities. The first issue was who to pay to stay out of the coop, and arrange for someone to do the cleanup duties. There was little money available and everyone was poor and close to starving. It was one of those times I appreciated my job.

It took me about fifteen minutes to meet the right person, who arranged these things for us.

Rich and I were now Considerados, which meant we had paid bribes in order to live a less complicated life. I also rented a very small space that was laughingly called a room. There were only six available rooms with just enough space to lie down and with a door that could be secured with a lock. It was minimal security but it was all there was. There was no roof over the room area for fifteen, maybe twenty feet above the top of the seven foot small wall. The wall was made of brick and held together with bed bugs, or so it seemed.

By paying a bribe I could have my wife visit and stay in the jail if she wanted to. The room was her spot so she could stay out of sight. I was uncomfortable with this arrangement because of the unpredictable nature of the environment but she did not appear worried, staying several days at a time. She said the hot plate restaurant had better food than the Acapulco restaurants she had found.

But when she was there I did not sleep. I would watch over her and my daughter, the one time she stayed the night. The bed bugs were so voracious I spent the nights keeping them off my family. My wife's restroom facilities consisted of a bucket in my room and my daughter wore diapers. After a short visit my protective instincts overrode my desire to be with them and I would not let them spend the night again. You live, and sometimes you learn.

The coop was at the far end of the complex, with restrooms on the entry side. There were two restrooms, one open to the people not locked in the coop and the other inside the coop. The restrooms were back to back, with a wall in between. There were seven toilets with a five gallon bucket and a faucet. You filled the bucket with water and poured it into the toilet to flush it. Toilet paper was left in a pile next to the toilet and it was always a tall pile. Immediately across from the toilet were the showers, three to four feet apart. There were seven or eight toilets across from the same number of showers. These facilities served a thousand plus people and were full of rats and feces. It was not a pretty picture.

I was a stranger in a strange land and I had never felt so alone and vulnerable in my life, nor have I since.

***

We had been inside less than an hour and I was already smoking a fat joint that cost me five pesos. If you had the means, every drug imaginable on the planet, both legal and illegal, was available. The favorite among the Mexicans was, by far, alcohol.

The place was a living nightmare and many people used drugs to escape it. I was among them although you had to be careful. Here's a case in point. I had been in a little less than a year and was bored, so I decided to drop acid and got off like gang busters. Then the jail was invaded by twenty, maybe twenty-five fully armed Mexican death dealing soldiers. This only happened once while I was there, and I chose that time to drop acid. What were my gods thinking? I guess they were bored, too. I sat back and watched the show. I did not imagine them, they were really there. One of the Americans, a little older than me, was getting off on my high – contact high – and wanted to climb the wall. They would have shot him if he tried. I had to take care of him. In my condition then I would have had trouble handling that. Shit happens when you least expect it and it pays to always remember that.

***

There was so little room in that place you had to more or less fight for a spot to sit, and sit there every day or you would lose it. The resident Gringos numbered less than ten and had a small area that was sort of open. They already knew we were coming thanks to the local newspaper. Being, understandably, a paranoid and suspicious group they did not trust us. Being busted with close to a ton made Rich and I number two in the volume department, which meant nothing to the resident Gringos.

The only small piece of comfort available was a simple deck chair. These chairs folded flat and had a cloth insert, and without them we would have been sitting on concrete all day, every day. Bed bugs infested everything, including the chairs.

We bought the chairs, clothes, bedding, and food through the window I described earlier. Nothing was provided for the inmates. Every morning there was a small army of boys who went to the market and picked up whatever the prisoners needed. The boys were honest and it was a good job for them, and paid better than laboring. They were careful to not make mistakes so they did not lose employment.

A small store was located at the entrance to the hallway where the six rooms were situated. One side had soft drinks and a few food items plus candy, and sometimes milk for sale. On the other side was a hot plate, three stool restaurant that served excellent food, fresh daily, mostly consisting of beans and rice plus two or three types of hearty soup. My wife said the fried fish was the best she had tasted in Acapulco. If you had the funds you could eat well.

***

Our second day had some unexpected drama. Friends of mine, a young married couple, were in Acapulco for the New Year's celebrations. The lady did something foolish and stuffed her bra with weed, and tried to visit me. They found it with a strip search. I had been there such a short time I did not yet know who I should talk to so the problem would go away and she was facing a year in prison. She was beautiful so would have been sexually abused in there. I couldn't allow that to happen to her so I scrambled, got lucky and made the deal. She was freed in less than twenty-four hours at a cost of two thousand dollars. In the long run this hurt me because I saw there was money to be made.

With all this bullshit going on the resident Gringos began to relax. They had been worried Rich and I were some sort of police, but cops would not attract attention in this way.

Life settled into a holding pattern. Rich and I drifted apart. He gravitated towards a gang of beach punks who spent their time trying to rip us off. They were led by a twenty year old double murderer of two Canadians, a married couple on vacation. I could not have been more disappointed in Rich's choice. I believe he was looking for personal protection but he made a poor decision. This person drained Rich of his money for basically nothing.

***

It was less than a month before the next negative situation arose.

Before I continue, I should say that most of the time it was peaceful, even boring. I have concentrated on the drama but it was not an everyday occurrence, although it did happen at semi-regular intervals.

My room was chosen to store the English library owned by the resident Gringos. It consisted of around five hundred books and was a nice selection of hippy learning literature. If you fell asleep while reading your book would be stolen and used for toilet paper. They always tore the pages from the last chapter first to keep you from taking the book back. It was not malicious, more that they were very poor and unable to buy toilet paper so they took advantage. Almost all the Gringos were better off than ninety-eight percent of the indigenous.

There were small riots from time to time, usually politically motivated. One cooked off mid-afternoon on the basketball court. Around two hundred beach punks were agitated over something – I still don't know what. When these things happened it almost always turned out to be the Gringos' fault. This was no exception, business as usual.

We, the Gringos, saw it coming and had piled most of our stuff in my room which was the first in a line of three behind the soda store. It didn't take long for them to start looking for us and blaming Gringos in general for whatever it was. Remember, the room's ceiling was over fifteen feet above the seven foot walls. Eight of us were crammed into that small space, along with our things and the books.

They had a large amount of ammunition in the form of empty soda bottles which started flying over the wall, hitting the opposite wall in my room and making shrapnel. We were dressed in shorts and maybe a t-shirt so this was having a worrisome effect. I had been there less than a month and had no weapon except for a pop flare. They are six inches long and very small, about the circumference of a thumb, with a string dangling from one end. You pull that to set it off, a single shot.

I was frustrated, and mad, and couldn't take any more of this bombardment. So I made my stupid little gesture. I knew who the leader of these punks was, Rich's best friend, the murderer. My plan was to try to hit him in the upper body, or the face. I opened the door and ran out to see them less than twenty feet away, two hundred strong. I stood firm and took my shot.

It totally missed, going over their heads and bouncing off the back wall. My heart sank. The flare was red, with a smoke trail and it gave a loud pop. It startled them and a shout went up that the Gringos had guns. They disappeared into the chicken coop and I was left standing alone with nothing but a spent flare.

The best defence is often offense, even if it is a long shot. Frankly, I could not believe it. In that place, I had to be larger than life to survive.

As far as being robbed went it was simple. When someone approached and made demands for your shirt, pants, belt, shoes, or money, all that was necessary was a firm, 'No'. They respected nerve and attitude. If they damaged you, charges would follow, but slowly. There was only one American killed while I was there. The way to comport yourself was with tons of self-confidence. I took shit from nobody. I was alone in there with no-one to watch my back but I walked like I owned the place. I was young and well trained and packed a potent punch. In other words, bullshit and attitude was what got me through. But it was the hardest time in my life.

***

Every four to six weeks the local cops would do a sweep of the surrounding beaches, looking mainly for those sleeping on the beach with not much spending money. There were usually around fifteen to thirty people arrested and thrown in with us.

Every time it happened a feeding frenzy would fill the air. We had all the petty criminals from Mexico City and Acapulco who were the ones who made the residents lives much harder. They seemed to have a running contest between themselves as to who could rip us off the most.

Around eight or ten at night the recent detainees would be thrown in jail. Whenever we saw large groups enter we would do our best to fade into the background. We could not attempt to warn or help the new victims.

If we did, we would suffer.

Those poor saps were a boost to the economy of the jail. No interference was expected from us. Robberies would be openly going on every twenty or thirty feet.

When you first enter jail you are nervous and unsure because of your total ignorance. All these people needed to do was say 'No' and the robbers would go to the next person. They were not looking for more charges, just easy marks. Almost all the detainees would give up whatever was demanded. For us, the exception and the most entertaining was the occasional 'No'.

After being robbed the new detainees would complain to the small group of Americans because we did not stand up and help them. They were thoughtless, or maybe stupid. We lived in that jail and would be there still after those fools had gone. Our lives were hard enough as it was. You learned this the hard way – as I did. In my first month I stood up and warned several new detainees who didn't take my advice and were robbed anyway, and I suffered for it.

***

The guards did nothing to police the inmates. They just kept us locked up.

Our police force came from other inmates. We had an elected president of the jail, which was a sought after position. He would get a piece of everything, all the drugs, alcohol, food, rooms, and anything he could attach a bribe to. Any person stealing had to kick back or suffer the consequences. For the petty rip-off they had a filthy, trash encrusted barrel. It was filled with water and the person being questioned was dunked head first in the barrel all the way to the bottom. They would let that person almost drown, then pull him up and question him, employing other torture tactics and threats.

The president had a crew of murderers working for him. Called Bastonaros, the badge they carried was a bull's dick tendon. It was around three feet, or a little less. The older bull tendons were the most effective. They worked just like a whip, taking a couple of layers of skin off an inch wide and three to six inches long with each hit. The name for these torture tools was chilies.

This threat pretty much kept the peace. They killed a few, but not many. It was either an accident related to alcohol use or too many offenses against the person and, usually, not paying the kick back.

The Gringo killed was, in my opinion, an accident. He was a doctor from California in his early fifties. As a small aside, if you travel to the third world and go crazy, or are already crazy, the outcome will be dire. They do not put you in a mental institution. That costs money. They jail you in a place that will make a fully sane person crazy.

I don't know what this man did to get the attention of the police but it must have been bad. They did not put him in the chicken coop, which left two other places. Walking around with us, spooking everyone out (how would you sleep with a madman about doing strange things?) or in the bartalena, a hell hole.

The bartalena is solitary confinement, an unbelievable place with human feces smeared on all the walls and the ceiling. It had at most a five foot ceiling which made it impossible to stand up straight, and had a five by five foot square floor space with a hole in it opening to a free flowing sewer which served as a toilet. Very little water was provided and almost no food. Nobody could live for very long on such a restricted diet.

The doctor was acting up and attracting all the wrong attention from the president and his henchmen. They drank every night to excess. Initially, what happened was a diversion that got out of hand due to the degree of inebriation. I am not sure what happened to start the beating that followed. I assume the doctor took a swing at the president that connected.

The president and his boys ran the bartalena, which was a key part of their disciplinary tools. No-one belongs in that torture chamber and we had to toe the line or suffer the consequences, and I and almost all the others did, to stay out. The only time I saw inside it was to remove the doctor.

When Gringos screw up they come and get the available Gringos to clean up the mess and I was one of the four chosen.

The doctor, after being beaten not too severely and left alone for an hour or two had taken all the shit – his and other deposits – and smeared it all over his entire body, even his eyelids. It was one of the most bizarre things I have ever seen. He was nude except for his chosen method of covering himself.

The four of us took newspapers and wrapped his flailing limbs so we could pick him up without getting all those feces on us – gross, to say the least. We carried him to the shower as he bounced like a trampoline. We did our best and somewhat cleaned him but he fought us every inch of the way.

After the cleaning job I went to the hotplate restaurant and bought a bowl of chicken soup, a nice sized chicken breast with chopped onion and cilantro, plus tortillas. It was a good meal and cost fifteen pesos. I took it back to him and he was still in the shower in the corner. He had the water flowing and appeared to be hiding behind the flow, like it was a force field. His face had a maniacal sneer on it that was disturbing, but I handed him his soup and hoped it would help, since he had not eaten since his arrival. He took the bowl, holding it in the spray of water, gave a guttural cackle and turned it upside down and smashed it on the floor. I had to pay for that bowl.

In our little world, we had done everything we could. The president's men took him back to the hole and we never saw him again. It's pure speculation as to what happened, and all I knew was that he died two days later, spending most of that time in the infirmary.

Two days after his death his young adult children came to the jail and demanded to speak to all the Americans in the population. The president was nervous because he knew that what happened could put him away for thirty years.

I was called first, not knowing what was waiting for me, and if I had I may not have sat down with the children, who were around my age. All the English speaking snitches in the prison were gathered close to the window so they could report on what was said.

The kids were crying, saying they knew he was beaten to death as there were huge bruises all over his body. Those bruises were not there the last time I saw him. They wanted me to tell them what happened.

That was not possible. If I did I would not have made it back down the hill, probably not even away from the window. This was one of the hardest things I have done in my life. I looked them in the eye and said, "Don't you see my position? Can't you understand? I cannot help you in any way. I do not know what happened."

When I got back inside I warned the other Americans about what was waiting for them. Each one made the decision not to go to the window. I still believe I was on the hit list for a while. I have never spoken about it again until writing it now.

***

That place could drive anyone crazy, if he wasn't before, and if he was already crazy it could tip him further down the rabbit hole. Picture a six foot naked Gringo with a full leg cast from his toes to his crotch. It's a bizarre picture, especially when you factor in that he has no crutches and is bouncing on his good leg, making his privates fly up and down.

As stated before, people, especially crazy, sometimes thought they were in a hot pink painted bar. This man was no exception. He started ordering drinks and sat down right across from me. It was a large, heavy white table. People slept on the benches. I have no idea why, but crazy people were drawn to me. This man was saying some reasonably coherent things along with the gibberish so I was not overly alarmed but was ready to run with little or no notice. The table had a medium sized plastic container sitting between us with some rock salt and several chilies in it. The table and five others were used to serve the so-called free food. You couldn't live on it as there were not enough calories or volume to sustain a person.

He stopped gibbering and reached out, picking up the plastic container. He stuck his other hand between his legs and came up with a handful of feces, and painted a ring around the container with it. Then he set the container back down with a satisfied expression. By that time I was at least twenty feet away, hopefully out of shit throwing range. It would have been funny if it weren't for the fact that he was sitting on the bed belonging to one of the president's men. That man, like almost all his men, was a murderer. Plus, the bed was freshly laundered because his wife was scheduled to visit the next day. The man was in the shower, not expecting the message he was about to receive. He came out with his face half covered with soap, totally naked. Now there were two naked people in the same confrontation. I was sure I would see a murder in the next five minutes but I did not, and the only reason for that was the death of the doctor a month or two earlier.

***

Here's another crazy person story.

The basketball court was where the people being locked in the chicken coop were lined up and counted at six in the evening, usually in a large spiral and in alphabetical order. The latest arrivals were counted last. The ones who paid to stay out of the coop were counted after the main body was taken care of. If you were really crazy you were not put in the coop but were left outside with the fifty to one hundred who paid for the so-called privilege.

I was in a line along the wall on the side of the basketball court, waiting to be counted. Across from me were the new arrivals, one of whom spotted the few Americans in-house, and began screaming damnation, directed at us. He was a small, slender and maybe one hundred and thirty pound person so we did not think him a threat. Other than entertainment he did not exist.

His problem, it seemed, was that he thought a Gringo sold him some bad acid. He was speaking Spanish and reasonable English. We gave him some verbal abuse and he didn't back down, but we ignored him and more or less forgot him.

With the count completed we went about our usual routine, not giving the crazy another thought. I went to my room to collect my soap and shampoo for the evening shower. I came out with nothing but a towel held across my body with one hand, and soap and shampoo in the other. As I left the short hallway in front of my room I saw the same small crazy person standing maybe fifteen feet in front of me with the cutting board from the hot plate restaurant in his hands. It was five or six inches thick, a little larger than a square foot, and weighed over ten pounds. As I stepped out the crazy person threw it sideways, using all his body weight and putting a lot of force behind it. Luckily, I had my arm across my body and that was where it struck me.

It took me down and I almost passed out. I was lying on the ground, fighting to stay conscious. My picture of the world had large black spaces spread out in my vision. This was the closest I have ever come to being knocked out. In the meantime, the crazy had armed himself with the large metal container used to bring the milk down, and it was heavy. He had it raised above his head, screaming and coming on the attack. All I could muster in my woozy state was to grip the cutting board and hold it like a shield with the little strength I had. Fortunately for me the crazy was tackled from behind by an alert friend and I was saved from serious damage, or even death.

It was hard for me to believe that an unexpected blow to the arm would incapacitate me to such a degree, and that a skinny, malnourished person could take me out. The only person on the planet who has accomplished that was that fool. I was a Marine, trained, and in good condition. He definitely got my attention.

As a result of this attack they put the crazy in the solitary hell hole for a month or more and failed to inform me when they let him out. I was sitting in my deck chair and caught an unusual movement over my left shoulder. I rolled out of the chair just as a four by four leg from one of the tables smashed my chair to pieces. I kept a stick one inch across and three feet long with me most of the time. I hit that crazy, hard, on his left arm between the shoulder and the elbow. It broke his arm and I no longer needed to worry about that crazy. The injury would take at least a year to heal.

I don't know why, but I was a magnet for the Crazy People. I had to be constantly on alert. I could tell you more stories about the crazies who wanted to kill me.

***

After three or four months in prison I had been told it would not be much longer until my release many times. The usual was a guarantee that it would be between three days and two weeks, for sure. At first, I was hopeful and believed it. That turned into disbelief and depression. The normal jail time for marijuana was three to eleven months no matter how much you were given. The system employed by Mexico was that if you received less than five years you were eligible for a Fianza. That meant you would receive a bond, a set price per month and times the number of years sentenced. That was the structure of the legal bribes.

You had to sign a book every month until your release date and then they gave you back your bond. Americans and anyone else not a Mexican national were deported. Once you left the country your bond was forfeit and the judge and your lawyer split the bond. It was legal graft and we were happy it was available. Then our dickhead President Nixon stepped in and paid a fifty thousand a month bribe to all Federal judges to always sentence any drug offence, especially marijuana, to more than five years.

This was the opening salvo to that ridiculous War on Drugs. My first sentence was five years and three months. I was the second American ever to be sentenced over five years for marijuana. A few months later it had risen to seven with word that it would soon be twelve.

I needed no further motivation to plan my escape.

My first ideas were lame at best.

I was looking for inspiration and not having any of those inspirational flashes. The first idea was a forty foot ladder made from the wooden frames of the deck chairs and held together with wooden dowels, consisting of twelve or so frames. I made a fifteen foot test model to see if it could hold a two hundred pound weight forty feet in the air. It would have been unlikely to succeed.

I made many small cuts in the walls, and bored several holes to peep and plan through. The only wall we could have cut through was on a street adjacent to another jail, Federal Prison. Army and Acapulco cops were in there in force at all hours of the day.

I smuggled in jewelers' saws. They are a foot long wire, encrusted with diamond dust. I attached a fifteen foot line to either end of the saw, wrapped the saw around the steel bars and from my cot fifteen feet away cut several of the bars. I could have kicked them out and crawled through.

I learned how to pick padlocks and bought identical locks to the ones the jail was using, smuggled them in, and used them to practice my skill, shortening the time needed to open them.

But my best idea was egg salad.

I was able to smuggle in odorless and tasteless pills that were powerful downers.

For several months I had been making egg salad for a late night snack, and it was to be the delivery system for the drugs. I gave a taco to both guards going in and coming out, so they would be used to accepting food from me.

The only time the guards had to walk through a small section of the jail with inmates was when they changed the rear guard tower. Depending on whether there was a full complement of men it was two or four hours on the tower. The fresh one went through first and the tired one came back. The plan was to dose the fresh one and give a clean taco to the one going to the guard house to rest. While on the towers, day or night, they blew whistles or horns, and shone flashlights. That was to see if the guards were awake. More about this later.

The next attempt was presented to me by another inmate I trusted a little bit. It did not sound or feel like anything more than theft. A guard had offered to take me out through the front entrance. Out of curiosity, I foolishly started negotiations with him and was immediately busted and moved to the Federal Jail across the street. It was a straight setup from the Warden.

The Federal Jail, unlike the one I had just left, was escape proof. It was clean, and everyone had a bunk. It was a totally different place. The people locked up in that jail were doing long sentences. The president and his men were serious and would not stand for any of the petty disturbances the other jail was chock full of. It made my time there like a vacation and almost pleasant.

The second or third night, at around midnight, I was taken out of my nine-man cell and transported a tad roughly to the basement to meet with the Warden. This was the time of day and the place where they did their murders.

Before I was even presented to the Warden they tried to make me uncomfortable but after the events of the last few months I did not frighten easily. If you did not keep your meager wits about you how could you make any move that became available?

I was seated at the end of a ten-foot table. The warden was at the other end, surrounded by the president and five of his most trusted murderers. The Warden's first statement was to the effect that if I tried anything like that again I would be killed.

I played the only card I had, expressing the obvious. They had me, there was nothing I could do to stop them but I could guarantee my friends on the outside would avenge my death and everyone involved would die. I delivered my statement with no expression or nervousness, and kept a steady cold stare.

I did not ask any questions, just sat and stared straight into the Warden's eyes. It was a serious bluff. My friends on the outside would not lift a finger to avenge me, but the Warden appeared taken aback and had nothing left to threaten me with.

I was returned to my cell and found out later that the Warden was not respected and I had gained a margin of respect from the president and his henchmen.

But the Warden could still kill me any time he chose.

There were two hundred and fifty bunks available and the population was kept to that number. It was strikingly clean. The cell I was in was overseen by one of the president's men. He seemed to like me and tried to befriend me, on instruction, I am sure. At any rate I grew to like him. He was more directly responsible for my safety than anyone else.

There was a Gringo beside me, a counterfeiter, eight years into a twelve year stretch. We seldom spoke and were not allies.

The jail was concrete and two storeys off the ground. The business window was two flights down, where the main guard posts were. There was a pay phone provided which was welcome, unlike the other jail which had no phone.

***

One day I was descending the last flight of stairs, on my way to the phone, when I witnessed a horrible scene. I was maybe ten feet from the floor where the window and phone were located. I had no idea what was happening, but an inmate was trying to climb through the window to get at one of the guards.

The guards were armed with Springfield bolt action 7.62 caliber rifles. Why you would do what this inmate was doing I had no idea. Maybe it was a suicide.

The guard stepped back and pointed the rifle at the inmate, with me in the background, and fired one shot. The inmate lifted, and fall backwards, dead, I think dead before he hit the floor. The bullet went through him and hit the concrete of the stairwell very close to me, showering me with bits of mortar. This had nothing to do with me and was one of those unlucky coincidences. If I had been three or four steps further down the stairs it is more than likely there would have been two casualties that day.

The loss that upset everyone was the phone. The bullet also passed through the pay phone and the telephone company was very slow to replace it.

***

I was in my nine-man cell with my new best friend (do read that tongue in cheek). This was the safest place for me to hang out. I made a deal with a chef from Mexico City and two others, plus my new friend, for meals prepared by the chef and paid for by me and one other inmate. I didn't have to clean the dishes or help in preparation, just order and pay for the food every other day. The chef was professional and brilliant at cooking on a hot plate. I looked forward to my meals.

***

In the nine-man cell there were three steel bunks three levels high. My bunk was on the third level, hotter but it made me harder to reach.

We were locked in from nine in the evening until six in the morning.

By this stage I had been there two weeks and was as comfortable as I could be in that situation. I had talked to everyone in the cell trying to get a read on what they were like, who they might be working for, and the level of sanity.

One was iffy, a Cuban who wore a red, full body jumpsuit. He was a double murderer and a political. Along with the suit he wore a red knitted woollen hat, marking him as a Communist. It is warm all year round in Acapulco and this guy's outfit made him stand out from the crowd and marked him as unstable.

It was when I was returning to my bunk from the restroom when the Cuban made an unexpected move, hitting me on the chin as hard as he could. This was a surprise move but was not effective. It was a challenge so I needed to react. After the punch the Cuban returned to his center bunk and pulled his legs up to his chest, for protection I guess. I was not upset until I felt my chin and realized I was bleeding and that pissed me off. I have never seen anything like his reaction. He seemed to shrink before my eyes and all I did was slap his legs that were still drawn to his chest.

My new best friend reacted quickly and called the president and his boys who had been drinking, as usual. They manhandled the Cuban out and down to the same room I was in with the Warden. Remember the description of the bull dick tendon, called a chili? They beat and whipped him for over two hours. It made him scream. We could hear every chili slap and every punch. This was far more than he deserved for his offense. I thought there was a history with this out of control person. He was making a point. If you get out of line again, you are dead.

It sent the message to the rest of the inmates, too. All through the jail you could hear every chili slap and every punch. My thought was *lucky me*, I did nothing to deserve this new notoriety. From that time on when I wanted to sleep during the day I had to have someone watch over me. You do not want a double murderer with an ax to grind focusing on you.

When I saw the Cuban a week later, after he spent time in the hole, he was still very much damaged, mostly chili wounds all over his face, and every inch I could see. He was missing at least one tooth.

***

As I have stated, that was a jail you could not escape from. I got busy finding out what the bribe would be to return to the other jail. I was informed I would spend at least six weeks there. The bribe went to the Warden - wonderful, my favorite person.

I had a lawyer talk to the Warden, along with others not in the legal profession. The Warden relented and allowed me to return. By that time he was part of the escape conspiracy and would be paid well.

The new attempt had been endorsed by the ruling political party. The main reason for their support was not because they cared about me in any way, but for the inmate who ran the jail to make money.

He had performed a service for them – the murder of the Governor of Geurrero in a parade with thousands of witnesses. In order to keep him alive and available for future jobs they gave him the jail to live in. It kept Cheo safe from retribution. He sometimes slept there, had a key to the jail, and a family in Acapulco. He was free to come and go as he wished.

To show how easy it was to leave Jail Number 2 if you were a Mexican national, I will tell you a quick story about the president at that time. Not the hitman, a minor jail official who was also an inmate.

He was driving the jail jeep, bright red with Jail No. 2 written all over it and was at a party, very drunk. He began starting trouble, with his forty-five, with the people attending the party and they called the cops. He jumped into the jeep and had a running gun battle with the police. The word is many shots were fired. He ran back to the jail and once inside the cops were powerless to charge him or do anything about it. I do not know how many people he hurt or how severely they were injured.

If you were Mexican and had money to pay, and were not yet sentenced it was relatively easy to get a permission/bribe from the Warden to leave the jail. His position was political and at the bottom of that ladder. He was ambitious and would not get involved in anything that might have hindered his rise politically, and that was why he was so worried about me and my plans.

I despised this vermin and wanted him to do some time.

This was one insane world I lived in.

For the Mexicans, it was normal, and they had no other choice but to endure. My heart went out to them, still does. They have no recourse and must persevere.

***

The only time I was stabbed was by a drunken friend. Anyone, when they drink to excess for several days will change and their face will become distorted. That was the way he looked at the time. He had family problems, perhaps, or whatever. So when he came at me in a darkened hallway he mistook me for someone else.

He had a point, not a cutting knife, but a tool made simply for killing someone by sticking them. In that jail there were many sharps, or pointed instruments of death, easy to get or to make. A real knife is called a cucheo.

He mistook me for someone else and tried to stick me with the point. I caught the point with my hand and received a small puncture wound. It wasn't deep, maybe half an inch.

After he sobered up he apologized every time he saw me. That happened in Number 2 before I was sent to the Federal Jail. I paid a fifteen hundred dollar bribe to be sent back to Number 2.

What a fitting name for that jail.

***

While I was gone Rich took over my other escape attempt and pretty much put my business on the street. I was more than a little pissed. Rich's best friend was the leader of the beach punks, the murderer. I hated him with a passion. He caused many problems for me as well as stealing most of Rich's money. Rich was a fool.

While I was gone my room was rented to someone else.

Rich's friend, the double murderer, was being released after only two years. He had a wealthy family who pulled strings and got him released. I was glad to see him go even though it was so unfair to his victims and their families. However, when people like him who hurt or killed someone inside were released they were usually dead a month or less afterwards. He was no exception. Out two or three weeks, he was on the phone talking to his mother when he was kidnapped. It turned out he was kidnapped by the cops. They tortured him extensively by cutting off his nose, ears, fingers, toes, and private parts. They did it to send a signal to all other thieves that people vacationing in Acapulco are not to be robbed or murdered.

It would, most emphatically, not be tolerated.

For months after his death his mother pleaded in every Sunday paper for whoever killed her son to please send the missing parts back to her so she could bury them. She never received them.

I thought it was fitting that he died in the manner he did, and it represented, after his death, what would not be tolerated.

An example of this that I experienced, not directly, but by being in the same place, was when I was sitting by a man who was watching the television that was seldom on. I heard a dull thunk, thunk, thunk, and did not know what it was. I was puzzled until I felt something wet on my face. It was dark, so I couldn't tell what it was, but it looked black. I glanced to my right and saw that man knocked out, being beaten from behind by another man who had a large lock on his finger and was whipping it back and forth, using most of his strength to really punish this man. He must have been knocked out with the first contact as he made no noise.

The injured man lived and got out a couple of days later. The one trying to kill him had waited until he was about to be released before making this attempt. He got out a month after his victim. He was out less than two weeks and was found sitting in his car at a stop sign, shot through the head.

It is a violent life in the third world.

***

I'll give you one more story on alcohol and how it changes people after its overuse and abuse – two best friends.

I had two acquaintances who were best friends. Something happened – long sentences, problems with families – I don't know. They drank, hard, for three or four days. Their faces had changed, as most do with an excess of alcohol, and they were belligerent. An argument broke out over who was the best friend to the other that progressed to a physical fight. One killed the other.

After the survivor sobered up and understood what he did he left, mentally. It was tragic, to say the least. Alcohol is an insidious, disgusting drug and should never be abused, or even used, in my opinion.

***

This is the next to last escape attempt.

As I stated before, I thought this one through thoroughly. It was a solid plan and it did work, but not for me.

My best friend in the Federal Jail used it to escape along with around thirty others. He paid to move to Jail Number 2 and made good his escape.

In my absence, Rich had told the Gringos about my escape plan and invited them to join. Five or six were for it and wanted to join. As you can imagine, the more people involved, the less likely it was to be successful. By that time the real escape attempt was coming together. It was solid and less of a physical risk. This was my choice, my chance, and I did not want anything to jeopardize it.

They felt that Christmas or New Year's was the best time. I was trying to dissuade everyone from making the attempt. It was Christmas week and every routine was disrupted. Plus, because of Rich, I had lost control. I did not make the final decision which was left up to a vote that decided on New Year's.

The mechanics of the attempt depended on drugging the guard on the back tower, using the tower to get to the top of the forty foot wall, then using the volleyball net to climb down the other side.

There was one barred gate between us and the tower. I had already cut several of the bars and the plan was to kick them out and crawl through, up the tower and over the wall.

I had been making egg salad for months. I gave away two tacos every night to the guards as they came to and from the tower so they became used to the delivery method for the drugs.

Against my wishes, New Year's Eve was when the attempt would take place. Nothing was normal at that time as there were extra guards on duty. I did my best to talk them out of it and wait until things returned to normal but they were determined to go.

I did the egg salad bit and drugged a man I had never seen before. He was older and not in the best of shape, which worried me as I did not want to hurt him or anyone else. Then one of the extra guards set his chair up where there had never been a guard. They must have called it holiday measures. He was looking straight at the gate we needed to go through, meaning there was no way we could make the attempt.

We now had an older guard dosed and in the process of passing out. All I could think of was that we would be busted and sent to the other jail, and never get to make the escape. I wanted to say 'I told you so' to the rest of the idiots, but what good would that do.

I could see the tower from my sleeping area. The guard hadn't passed out, but he wasn't moving, either. Do you remember what I said about their methods of checking the guards aren't sleeping on duty – whistles, flashlights, horns? If there was no response they would go and shake the guard awake.

Before long there was no response and they tried for thirty minutes to wake the guard from a distance, but he did not respond. Then the head guard climbed the tower and banged on a piece of metal right by the passed out person's head, and he did not respond. I was very worried he would not wake again.

They tied a rope around his chest and began to lower him the forty feet. Just before his feet hit the ground he woke up and started wailing about being hung over, and how he'd partied too much the last week.

They never suspected foul play and did not ask a question of one single prisoner. It sounds weird, but that's how it happened. Go fucking figure…

After a couple of weeks I started to breathe again.

Next up, the real escape.

Acapulco Escape

The only reason I was still in jail was that I refused to leave without Rich. It was my code to never leave a partner behind. I had been told I would have left six months earlier if I went alone. But we came in together and we would leave together, even though we were no longer friends or even allies. We took divergent paths from the very first day. Rich made fast friends with the beach punks led by that double murderer of two Canadians (which he paid for with his murder after his early release). Rich's friendship with this despicable person drove a wedge between us, plus, I think, he felt guilty about leaving the truck on the highway and putting us both in prison. He wanted separation from me, and the guilt that seeing me each day would have kept fresh, and I'd had enough of him. There was no love lost.

As I related earlier, the man who ran the jail, a political murderer of the Governor of Guerrero named Cheo, stood to make a very nice payday by setting up the escape. Without his involvement, I would probably have done all my time.

Everything was set and ready to go. I had one last meeting with Cheo who gave me a choice of backing out or proceeding, and explained that if I did not make it I would see him one last time. Cheo would kill both Rich and myself because we knew too much and could make problems for his employers.

That was sobering and I spent a short time with Rich asking if he was willing to risk it or stay and do his time. I was going, with or without him. He thought about it for maybe thirty seconds and agreed with me. The die was cast.

It was about seven weeks after the New Year's sad attempt. We were not told which day it would be. There was a public address system for calling prisoners up to the window, or to Court, or for short term visits. Obviously, no guard wanted to come down and collect us personally.

That morning they whispered over the loudspeaker system for the people going to Court to come. It was strange, as aside from the whispering over the loudspeaker it was six in the morning and no-one went to Court before nine. Rich and I were expecting the attempt but had no directions or indications of when. This being out of the ordinary we slowly walked to the exit where a guard was nervously trying to hurry us up. Another guard stopped us and started to ask why we were there but his fellow guards were quick to caution him to let us pass.

We went through the two or three locked and barred gates, and arrived on the street between the two jails. We saw five policemen with brand new uniforms, and a gray Dodge rent-a-car. I would have had them wash the uniforms five or six times before the escape. All they lacked was the price tags dangling like an old country performer called Minnie Pearl.

We piled into the car and were whisked away. The five were brothers of a very good friend of mine. They took Rich and me to a house not too far away. We changed clothes and I shaved off a red beard that had been growing for the last six months. If there were pictures I hoped the absence of the beard would throw them off.

At this point, I made changes in the escape route and the general method of escape. That was to confuse the people selling the escape. I did not trust them completely and didn't want them to know where Rich and I were. I had four different vehicles plus a small four place aircraft to work with. We went south to go north, driving all day the first day to northern Oaxaca, all on small gravel roads.

There was a serious military checkpoint at the Acapulco city limit on the road to Mexico City. There was no way around it, we had to go through. We were in a Volkswagen Beetle, with me in the back and Rich up front with our driver. The soldiers were suspicious and did a walk around, looking closely for anything out of the ordinary. This car, luckily, had louvers over the back window, and I say luckily for reasons which will soon become apparent. After ten minutes or so they flagged us through.

We traveled a short distance and I, for some reason, began looking around the back seat. I looked over into a small well behind the seat and spotted a forty-five lying there in plain sight. I think I understand why it was left there. I believed then that it was placed there by someone who wanted me to fail, and in retrospect I know that was the purpose. We were not supposed to make it out of Acapulco. I will say more on this later.

They changed cars and we were now in a Volkswagen bus, and turned south. The other three cars went north, and spaced out several hundred miles apart on the route. That meant Rich and I would have three more car exchanges before we hit the border.

We drove all day on gravel, south to a small town at the end of the road. There was a classic, very short, missionary airstrip there. It was up a mountain at a ten to fifteen degree angle and had a small valley across the lower end and another mountain directly across from it. It was necessary to bank right or left immediately after becoming airborne. When landing you had to flare and touchdown, then apply full throttle to climb to the top of the strip. It was vital to make the landing on the first try because it would have been almost impossible to go around without hitting the mountain. It was necessary to land and take off into the wind. On strips like that it was only possible to land up the mountain and take off down it and would almost always be a cross wind landing. I used several strips like that one in my smuggling operations in later years.

We arrived at dusk and parked well up the strip. The small town was a mile away. Nobody was at the strip and I hoped Rich and I hadn't aroused anyone's curiosity.

The elevation was around eight thousand feet, making it chilly. We slept in the van that night, and the four place single engine aircraft was supposed to be there one or two hours after sunup. Sleep did not come to me. I was awake and alert for the duration of the escape. My antennae was active, obviously more in tune to the danger than my conscious was.

We sent our driver to town in search of a good meal to share and he came back with an outstanding one. It came complete with fresh blue tortillas. There were beans and rice, and a very good beef steak. The meal was much appreciated by everyone.

That night we had a clear view of the sky, with several planets almost in a line coming up over the horizon. I was taken by the coincidence and appreciated the visual effect. The almost magical feel of the day was overwhelming. I had the feeling that if I wanted to, I could have told everyone I came into contact with that we had just escaped jail and it would not have made a difference. In other words, it was our time to make this move. We had filled that space and it was time for other directions that would, hopefully, be more positive.

Rich and the driver were asleep on the front seat but I was awake and on guard, as I would remain until I was safely home. It was around five in the morning when a noise came from the base area of the strip. It sounded like animals, probably horses. I still had the pistol that was planted in the other vehicle at the checkpoint, so I retrieved it from its hiding place and woke Rich and the driver.

Whoever it was approached at a slow pace. Rich, the driver and I moved quietly into the foliage behind the vehicle and observed two men, dressed in casual clothes but with police badges and cuffs, dismount and start a slow inspection of the vehicle.

At the right moment, I announced my presence by cocking the forty-five and getting control of the situation.

At my instruction, Rich disarmed the cops and used their handcuffs to make sure they were no longer a threat. I placed them back to back and wrist to wrist. They could not move or run quickly.

The sun was just starting to peek over the horizon and there was little time to complete this improvisation. I made the cops swallow two downers apiece, marched them up the mountain around a mile, and looked for a ravine with a tree to cuff them to. The drugs were already beginning to take effect.

The horses were left tied close to the cops. I needed about two hours before they were found. The plane was expected in an hour or less. The driver was instructed to drive back down the only road to the next town, find a place to stash the VW, call the cops and tell them where to go to pick up their boys, then take a bus.

I seem to be a magnet for extreme drama.

Before sunup the airstrip began to bustle with activity. People driving their cars up and down the rough runway was puzzling. There were few cars in the pueblo as mostly burros, horses and mules were the modes of travel. There were maybe thirty people on the strip now, possibly waiting for other flights or maybe just interested in the two Gringos who did not belong. There were no other Americans in the village.

The aircraft arrived, maybe an hour late. I was very happy when it made a safe landing. I did not know this particular pilot but he had a good reputation and was hired to transport goods and people in and out of the mountains. The men who flew those mountains were very good at their jobs. They did not last long if they were not.

The pilot knew what had happened the day before and agreed to take Rich and me to his home strip close to Izucar de Matamoros, but no further. That was in the state of Puebla, still well south and east of Mexico City. It was just out of the area where there would be many checkpoints looking for us. At Izucar we would be only about one hundred and fifty miles closer to the States after driving over ten hours south and flying two hours north. We still had about nine hundred miles to go.

When we arrived in Izacur, one of the cars sent north was waiting for us. We jumped into it and left at speed as it's harder to hit a moving target. I chose the gulf coastal roads because there were two running north and they were not far apart. We were beginning to think this would be successful. We were not complacent, but some comfort was creeping in.

We were heading for Tuxpan on the gulf coast north of Veracruz. We had successfully made the jump from the Pacific to the Gulf of Mexico. Rich and I changed cars in Tuxpan and went north to San Fernando, where we made our last car exchange. It was one hundred miles to the border in Brownsville, Texas.

We arrived in the other Matamoros just across the river from Brownsville, still in Mexico. It took two days to reach this point and was late at night. It was three days total since the escape. There was no cover traffic on the international bridge so I decided to wait until the early morning rush and get lost in that.

Rich made his own way from that point and I did not see him again for at least ten years.

I walked over the bridge with no problem from the Mexicans, and, elated, crossed into Texas. They asked if I was bringing anything back and I replied with a huge grin, "No, sir, just a case of the clap."

I went looking for a cheeseburger, typical Gringo!

Then it was off to the bus station to buy a ticket to Austin, and while waiting I ran into two Americans who were smuggling birds. They had just crossed the river, either by walking or by taxi. I was in the bus station watching them take the animals off their bodies. I don't know how many died but there had to be a few. I would guess around thirty birds. This is not something I favor. Regardless of your place in life you should try not to harm any living thing.

I boarded the bus feeling safe for the first time.

The Brownsville bus to San Antonio was uneventful. I changed buses for the Austin leg. At this time, the bus was empty with the exception of eight or so Mexican men, the bus driver, and me. My antenna was aroused. I was not sure why but I paid close attention to these Mexicans.

***

And now we are up to the part that began this chapter. I will continue from the part where I exited the restroom.

I could tell the driver was upset, because like me, he did not know what was going on. He witnessed everything but did not report it in San Marcos. I sat right behind him and waited until we were several blocks from the Austin bus station. The driver was as freaked as I was. We had not spoken to each other until I asked the favor.

I told him that I didn't know what the Mexicans were up to, but could he please let me off in traffic and I would be forever in his debt. What I asked could have cost him his job. He never said a word, but popped the door and I ran out as he closed it and drove on. The Mexicans were caught off guard and pressed their faces to several of the bus windows, watching me walk the other way.

The only explanation I have for this strange behavior is that because of the extreme reaction in Acapulco over the escape, they, the Political Party, sent a squad of kidnappers after me.

The army used my escape as an excuse to declare martial law and take over Acapulco. They locked up over six hundred city cops and most of the jail guards, plus that damn Warden. I think they locked up a few others for good measure.

If they took me back, and showed my dead body, claiming I was the only person responsible for this huge problem it would have given everyone an excuse to stop the army investigations, and everything would have returned to normal.

My wife was at home, and thanks to a good friend, she knew I was in the process of escaping for maybe one day before she got the call to come a short distance to pick me up.

I could not inform her because I did not know when it would happen, and this was the days before cell phones so no way of notifying her afterwards.

I did not want her to pick me up in Brownsville because I would have been waiting five or six hours, and I didn't want her involved in any way just in case something went wrong.

And as you saw, things did go wrong, although in the end it was successful.

I spent the next year in full culture shock, and constantly looking out the window for kidnappers.

My time in that jail changed me forever. I have only scratched the surface of my time there, as it would take up too much of this book to tell more. Instead it will be a separate book, *Escape from Acapulco.*

One thing is sure. That fucking place still calls.

Chapter Nine

The marijuana plant has long and strong fibers that make it excellent for the production of paper

Copilot

As time went on my business grew and I needed different ways to transport my loads. I also had to adapt to the changes brought about by the US Government's 'War on Drugs' and that meant more frequent, longer trips to places like Colombia. I was always learning new ways of doing things, new skills, and I was dealing with new people.

On one occasion I was in Louisiana, training to fly second in command on a Lockheed Lodestar, a plane well known as being excellent for smuggling marijuana, or taking skydivers up to throw themselves out. Obviously, we were not taking skydivers on our trips. The Lodestar was a large, twin-engine World War II vintage aircraft. Although a large plane it needed a relatively short runway, and it could move pretty quickly.

We were heading to the northern edge of Colombia and would be bringing back two tons of marijuana. This particular airplane felt like a tank and was reassuringly well built. We were about to discover just how well built it was.

The pilot in command was much older than me, and correspondingly more experienced. He was an excellent crop duster. We were using Jim's private airstrip, one he had been using for the last thirty years, mainly as a crop duster. The strip was short, two thousand feet in length and with no obstructions. It was surrounded on three sides by cornfields and on the fourth was bordered by a creek. It was situated in southern central Louisiana, less than one hundred miles from the Gulf of Mexico.

The Lodestar needed three thousand feet for both and landing and take-off to be safe, which posed a bit of a problem. It wasn't possible to lengthen the runway because the land around the strip was owned by a large farming operation which was not interested in selling Jim any land.

Undeterred, we were practicing landings and take-offs. Jim calculated the amount of fuel needed for five take-offs and landings. The aircraft was empty, except for the two of us. Because of the weight of the airframe and the sheer size of the aircraft – it was like flying a tank – it had an enormous amount of drag. It was long, tall, and wide.

We had made four successful take-offs and landings and were on a low approach for the fifth. We had full flaps and gear down, the highest amount of drag possible because to stop we needed every foot of available strip.

At two hundred feet one engine ran out of fuel and the one still running pulled us into a radical ninety-degree bank. There was no time for conversation, comment, or to make a plan. The plane was going down and we had to act instantly. There was one pilot in command and it was not me. The control surfaces of the plane were operated by muscle power. Jim was wrestling the left wing up, trying to get it back to level before we hit the ground. I was bringing the gear up, and the large flaps, trying to clean us up and prepare for the inevitable crash. Our actions were pure reflex. There was no time to even think about what might happen.

Jim managed to haul the left wing up so we were almost level when the tip hit the ground and we spun slowly through a cornfield. The corn was almost ready for harvest and very tall and that served as lubrication and a buffer. The propellers hit and were bent, plus one gear door was ripped off and the left wingtip damaged where it hit. Other than that, scratched paint and minor dings were the extent of the damage. Jim and I were shaken up and bruised. We exited swiftly, the potential for an explosion and fire, as always, at the front of our minds. That is the first thing to do in any crash – get out and get away from the plane. There was little fuel left on board so only a small chance of a fire, but we acted as though it was carrying a full load. You should always do that. You do not want to be burned.

As we walked away Jim looked at me sheepishly and said, "I made a miscalculation."

"I agree," I replied.

We laughed, a sickly kind of laugh, releasing the tension and adrenalin. We both knew we were fortunate.

***

Once we recovered from the shock our immediate problem was getting the plane out of the cornfield and into Jim's hangar. He had an old friend who was a mechanic who worked on this type of aircraft in World War II. It took him two, maybe three months to make it airworthy again, and he did an outstanding job. He was paid a fat bonus for his trouble.

Finally we were more or less prepared for the Gulf and Caribbean crossing. The Lodestar could not take off fully fuelled from that short strip but Jim was determined to use it. He thought there would be more risk from the Federal police than it was making the landing on his strip. The local police would not bust Jim and if they knew the Feds were after him they would warn him. He was a home boy and had lived there for over sixty years.

We loaded enough fuel to make the short trip to another, much larger, controlled airport. We would top up there and turn south for Colombia. The Lodestar was fast for its size and cruising speed was over two hundred knots per hour. It would take us around fourteen hours down and back, if we were not delayed for some unforeseen reason in Colombia or the weather did not take a turn for the worse.

Jim had made this trip several times in the past, and so far had bought his return fuel in Colombia. In this we differed as I always carried my return fuel with me. I preferred to cover any foreseeable problems myself and that is most likely the main reason I am still above ground.

We flew with no navigation aids whatsoever. We tracked out of a fifty thousand watt radio station and adjusted our course left or right to maintain the desired heading, crabbing into the prevailing wind. We would do the same thing on another radio station out of Cancun, Mexico.

We arrived in extreme northern Colombia and landed in an area without any towns, small or large. The airport had a restaurant, a small ten to twenty room hotel, and two bars. It must have had many planes visiting weekly. Obviously it was government protected as there were uniformed soldiers placed in prominent, highly visible, strategic positions. It was weird, I felt protected and threatened at the same time. This was not a place to hang out in for any length of time. It was a place to get your business done and leave.

Our load was waiting, which made me very happy. We fuelled, loaded, and left in less than an hour.

Flying off a signal provided by this facility we got our heading for Cancun. From Cancun we flew to Lake Charles where it was easy for Jim to find his small strip. We were low on fuel, as planned, so we were as light as possible for the length of the strip. We had two tons of extra weight on board so it would be, at best, a dicey landing.

Jim was an excellent pilot and he set the plane down smoothly, but had trouble stopping. The plane kept trundling on and on, and it felt like it would not stop until it hit something and the something looming was not a good thing to hit. Finally, we came to a stop less than twenty feet from Jim's ten thousand gallon fuel tank.

That was an experience I could have done without.

I did Jim's marketing for him which gave me two paychecks on this short – copilot and sales.

I found a cash buyer and wrapped up the deal in a week.

Except for the unexpected crash this trip was relatively uneventful.

We survived, there were several doses of adrenalin, there was a hint of danger, and I got paid.

I was still hooked.

Chapter Ten

Clothing made from hemp is as soft as cotton but stronger and more durable

Scoring Weed

I don't know if it was the same for everyone involved in my business, but for me the trials and tribulations of procuring and transporting pot always seemed to be strenuous.

On this occasion I was with two different groups of smugglers. One was looking for four hundred kilos (0.44 ton) and the other was pretty much unlimited, and was for three tons or more for this trip.

The first one was an old acquaintance of mine nicknamed BJ. The second one was a far more serious person from the valley of Texas. His name was Albert, that would be Al. He was touchy about his given name.

Neither one of them was overly bright.

We were in southern Mexico, in the state of Oaxaca. To be more specific, we were at the Istmo de Tehuantepec. We were to be working with people I did not know and were to be introduced by a Vietnam vet who lived in the area.

We arrived at the designated spot in an isolated spot in Oaxaca. There was no city within fifty miles in any direction. We left our vehicles just off the road and out of direct sight of the highway.

Our guide and the vet were supposed to provide us with horses or mules, or at the very least burros. While the guide and the vet were waiting for us, no animals were present. It was only a small change in the plan but was irritating as we could not move faster than we could walk and that made us more vulnerable. It meant we would be in the mountains longer than anticipated and that proved to be a factor, later on.

We walked for ten kilometers, just over six miles, with the guide. The mountains were breathtakingly beautiful. The view was incredible, verdant, tall green grass and trees as far as the eye could see. There were no power lines or any other sign that the area was even populated. It looked like nobody had ever set foot there.

The trail was well kept. It was the only means for the local Indians to travel in and out to buy supplies. When it rained the trail washed away in certain narrow spots. All the families living close pooled their labor and fixed any problem. It reminded me of a rural interstate, only narrower and in better shape than our roads.

Small, grass roofed houses with dirt floors were the only structures I saw. They were spaced a mile or two apart. The area was sparsely populated, and that plus the climate and soil made it perfect for the growing of our product.

Travelling down the trail we noticed whole families – mother, father, and children, lined up in a sort of stair-step formation, waiting for us to pass. I felt like we were in a parade; a parade of curiosity.

How did they know we were coming?

I call this the drum and it is a little spooky, the way the people in these isolated places know things.

We arrived at a small grass hut which was the meeting place. The head man and two of his lieutenants were waiting. When we entered the hut we found a pile of burlap bags full of immature marijuana which was not what we were looking for. The sample we were shown was what we expected, truly excellent. This was what was called a bait and switch.

When we entered the hut there were three or four Mexicans in total, but when we exited things were different. Waiting outside, looking nervous, were at least ten more armed people, surrounding the hut and us. Their weapons were not the best, all older shotguns, rifles and pistols. We were five Gringos with only two of us armed with pistols. I did not have one. We were in a poor position.

We grabbed the head man and stuck a 9 millimeter under his chin, stating we would shoot him, which was pure bluff.

Then the argument started. They said we owned the product in the hut and the only way we could leave was to pay in full. Not being complete idiots, we had no money with us. Rule number one – never bring money directly to the score. The money changes hands in another location.

It got angry and emotional for the next hour or two until I finally reached a tentative agreement. There was supposed to be two thousand kilos, so two thousand dollars or we begin shooting each other. It was a straight up rip-off.

The head man could not afford to walk away empty handed as his people would probably shoot him. A two thousand split fifteen or twenty ways would save face.

The next problem was that we did not have two thousand on the five of us, but one did have money stashed in his vehicle. That person was BJ. He left and made the trek down and back, taking hours on foot.

By then it was dark, with no moon. We had progressed to the point of passing a mescal bottle around and had relaxed as much as one could when surrounded by at least fifteen armed people forming a circular firing squad.

BJ returned with the bribe and came walking out of the darkness carrying a weapon I had not seen before.

There was the *click-clack* of everyone cocking their weapons, a sound like crickets on steroids in the stillness. All it would have taken for everyone to start shooting was one person to squeeze off a round. I was looking for a hole to crawl into.

Luckily, before that happened one of them saw that the weapon BJ carried was not the machine gun they thought, but a .30-30 lever action rifle. They laughed, a sick laugh, but a laugh nonetheless and much better than the alternative.

We paid the bribe and left with nothing.

I found out later that this was a family from Michoacan who had been run out of that state for just this type of business.

***

We walked out that night and I thought it was over, but not so.

The next day the gunman from the valley, Al, was very upset and wanted to shoot BJ, the person who brought that rifle. There was no reason to bring another weapon into such a tenuous situation. Stupid isn't a strong enough word for such an irresponsible action that nearly cost all of us our lives.

We were in my truck and Al had his 9 millimeter out and pointed at BJ's head.

I counseled restraint and convinced Al how wrong it would be, that no matter how angry he was over such a stupid move BJ did not deserve to die for it.

We parted ways and as far as I know, no-one involved ever worked with either Al or BJ on any other trip, ever again.

The trials and tribulations of procuring and transporting pot were endless.

Chapter Eleven

Hemp plastic is safe, recyclable, and biodegradable

Hiring Others to do My Work

At this point I had been in action in this business for over ten years and I was worn down. The pressure from planning, executing and trouble shooting smuggling operations was enormous. I lack the words to properly convey the level of responsibility I felt for my co-workers and their families. That was why I did as much as I could by myself. It was exhausting.

In the beginning, I was fortunate to have several competent people to guide me. By this point the majority of my fellow workers were in it for the money and for the most part were not as competent as I had come to expect.

The ones who did not get directly involved were the worst. They were the ones who got people killed or imprisoned with little thought except for the money they had invested. They did not take all aspects of the operation into account because they did not have any skin in the game. They, as a group, were delusional about the importance of their contributions compared to the people wo did the actual work. The workers were by far the most important, and they made the least.

To me, this is an indictment of the capitalist ideology worldwide, Workers Unite. Granted, if you are manufacturing autos or something else you have little chance of dying or going to jail because of your job, but it is still the ideology of capitalism that leaves the ones who do the work as the lowest paid, even in smuggling.

When I first started I moved dozens of truckloads of marijuana from deep in Mexico to the Rio Grande. The average one way distance was one thousand to fifteen hundred miles and the truck would usually be full. The pay was $1000 a run. The produce in the truck was worth $150-200 thousand. If, as driver, you were stopped or had an accident you would be imprisoned for a large chunk of your life, or possibly killed, depending on the cops who apprehended you. If they wanted to steal your load you would be dead. They did that to cover their asses so there was no worry about repercussions for their theft.

***

So, I was tired, and becoming disillusioned about my fellow smugglers. In need of a break I hired two so-called professional pilots for a trip out of Guerrero. They were supposed to be proficient in doing airdrops. One of them had taught the other how to fly and would be the pilot on command. I am sure, from hard surface runway to hard surface runway he was competent, but smuggling was almost never that easy. In smuggling you used improvised strips, quickly and cheaply built by non-pilots and with many unseen dangers.

One of the rules that kept me alive was that I would not land on any new strip I had not walked. It was imperative the pilot in command familiarize himself with the topography and possible obstructions before landing, and verify the length. All components had to be checked out if the pilot was to minimize risks.

The strip they were supposed to use was a twenty-four hour walk into the mountains one way. That made it potentially a four day trip to verify the strip. Gringos stand out, especially in the mountains. A target for many reasons, it was dangerous to expose themselves in that fashion.

However, I emphasized the importance of verifying the strip. The new pilot in command refused. I should have ceased negotiations there and then. But the load was already bought and on the strip. The growers misrepresented – possibly lied – about the distance from the nearest road to the strip, or perhaps had no way to judge it. If I hadn't been so fatigued I would have flown it myself after taking the necessary time and trouble to verify it.

To this day it troubles me that I did not take the necessary due diligence to guarantee success. I have a strong work ethic and sense of responsibility for others. The events of this trip would have been avoided if I had done it myself.

The trip was supposed to be an airdrop. The pilots had the parachutes and bags necessary for the volume. I had a friend with a five thousand acre ranch less than fifty miles from Austin. He agreed, for a fee, to allow the drop onto his land. I was to be in the ground crew plus several other workers. The main problem with an airdrop was that the product got strewn about and this was a night operation, therefore locators for each package were necessary.

I planned the trip so I could give the Mexicans a window on a certain day and time to expect the aircraft to arrive in Mexico. There was no way to contact the southern ground crew directly while in flight.

All my operations in Mexico and other countries did not have fuel available. To ensure you had the right octane that was not contaminated with water was imperative. You carried a double load inside the aircraft.

In other words, you had a flying bomb under your hands with any crash guaranteed to be explosive. The fuel was in modified fifteen gallon plastic containers. Refuelling meant sticking the neck of the container into the opening for the fuel tank, bring it up until it was upside down and using a large knife to poke holes in the bottom of the container to facilitate the flow. This was the most efficient method of transferring fuel, plus spillage was cut to almost nothing.

Under pressure from the growers I gave the go ahead, with complaints to all involved.

The trip was planned so everyone had their date and time for the beginning to the airdrop and the end.

The aircraft left on time and arrived at the strip on time, as verified by the growers. The so-called professional pilot made his approach to landing as though he had unlimited landing distance. He came in high and burned through at least a third of the strip before the gear touched the ground. The strip was covered with foot long slick grass. When he applied the brakes the aircraft hydroplaned on the long grass which made the brakes useless. He skidded off the runway and struck a rock with the prop before stopping. The damage was not fixable and the aircraft was rendered useless. It was an amateurish, stupid mistake.

I was at the ranch where the airdrop was supposed to take place. The time for the airdrop came and went. I waited all night, thinking the worst. It took the pilot three days to get to a phone. I was glad to hear they were alive and in good shape but had to wait for their return to hear the story.

There were problems getting them out of Mexico without papers. There was a paper check around fifteen to thirty miles from any border crossing. Without papers they would be arrested. However, I had the right connections and got them out of the country.

I finally got the full story a week after the crash. I was pissed off, and did not have an immediate solution.

The two pilots came up with a solution. They claimed they could get another aircraft, plus buy a prop to replace the damaged one and that they had the knowledge to do the work required on that remote Mexican mountain. I thought that unlikely but I was involved and could not leave the damaged plane where it was. The army would come to investigate and all the Mexicans and Indians involved would have been at extreme risk. They had camouflaged the fuselage as best as they could and everyone in the area knew what happened and were gossiping about it. The army was, I guess still is, ruthless and would torture and kill everyone they felt was involved. They did not care about making a bust, just shutting down and eradicating this growing operation.

I was extremely worried.

***

The crew of Indians stuck on the mountain with the damaged plane and marijuana had run out of supplies and had to make a trip to replenish beans and rice, plus other items.

The head man and his second in command were in a small town at the base of the mountains. A young man, and proven snitch, was in the head man's house asking questions. My friend and his partner were harmed with knives, nothing more lethal.

Suddenly the house was surrounded by the local cops. My friend and his second in command killed the young man and ran out the back of the house, trying to escape. The cops fired many shots and killed the second in command, and hit my friend. He spun around and went down. The head cop leaned over him, inspecting him to verify if he was alive or dead. He jumped up, killed the cop and made a getaway.

Now, because of incompetent pilots, there were three dead individuals involved in this screwed up operation. I did not know this, since there was no way to communicate with the head man who was on the run for his life. I never heard from him again and assume he was caught and killed.

The family of the head man contacted me months later and informed me about what had happened.

***

Other people who lived close to the strip where the crash occurred were still on the job. They knew the pilots were coming back to repair and remove the plane and waited daily for their return.

After about two months the two California pilots finally got themselves ready for another try. The Indians harvested more product and were willing to load both aircraft with the guarantee from me that they would be paid.

The airdrop was no longer possible and I had to provide a strip secure enough to allow the double off load of two aircraft. I had a ranch road on a large ranch not too far from Beeville, Texas. The road was wide with almost no obstructions. One of the workers on the ranch was helping to coordinate.

I always had a Plan B and C, and always had alternate strips within a forty-five minute drive from the primary. A, B, and C. Strip B was an old World War II concrete auxiliary strip. There were no buildings or any sort of support and no-one working there to help cover this offload. We would have to cut a wire fence and drive a quarter mile to the strip and aircraft.

Strip C was a student practice strip for the Airforce with a control tower and security guards. It closed operations at sundown. It was never supposed to be used except in a dire emergency.

These triple options came about because of my extensive experience and problems encountered in the past. I had never needed a third choice, but made sure one was available just in case. I checked these three strips daily before we launched this operation.

The California pilots took their time getting ready, tools, the prop, and the second aircraft. They claimed to be ready and began the second attempt. Our ground to air radio was short range so that we needed to be within thirty miles to communicate.

The pilots claimed they could make the prop exchange in less than one day, timing the return to be back by dark, or just after. I had not seen A strip in three days but the last time I checked it was sleepy as usual.

They timed their arrival for just after sun up. The second landing was successful because the pilot in command followed my instructions. He made a low approach and made contact with the ground as soon as possible after crossing the leading edge of the strip. They worked all day but could not complete the task. They left late in the day and were scheduled to arrive close to the expected hour in Texas.

I arrived at the ranch road strip at the appointed time to get a huge surprise. They had set up a drilling rig for oil exploration. It was right next to the road and made the road unusable, with at least thirty people coming and going with equipment for the rig.

When a trip has trouble involved it never seems to right itself and become a success, but this one took the cake!

I got on the ground to air radio, trying to raise the aircraft. Then I saw it, on its final approach to the temporary strip. The pilots had not tuned the radio to the correct frequency.

For some unfathomable reason they did not see the drilling rig and mountains of equipment on the road, plus the ten or so vehicles, until they were at less than two hundred feet. They buzzed the drilling rig and finally continued.

I spoke directly to one of them on the radio and made sure he knew to proceed to the secondary strip. It would take me and the other driver forty-five minutes to get in position. Myself and the other driver left in our two trucks and hustled to get there, arriving in just over thirty minutes. I was on the radio trying to raise the aircraft as we drove along a road running close to the concrete strip. The only boundary between us and the strip was a barbed wire fence. The strip had cattle on it and a large volume of manure all over it. There was no aircraft in sight and nothing on the radio as I tried to raise them once again.

They were nowhere to be seen, and were not within radio range. I began speculating; maybe they were low on fuel, or having mechanical problems. The backup driver and I waited for over thirty minutes and I decided to check C strip just in case, to cover all possibilities. I left the radio with the backup driver along with bolt cutters and other necessary pieces of equipment to do his offload if they finally showed.

It took another forty minutes to get to the military strip. It was dusk, but light enough to see well. That meant there would be personnel still on the strip. It was laid out in the shape of a large V, two strips, both a mile and a half long. To use it you had to taxi on the strip itself as there were no taxi ways.

The entrance was at the far end of one runway. There was a guard gate, but no guards on duty. I stopped at the gate and got out of my vehicle to scan the horizon, looking for any aircraft that might be in a landing pattern. There was nothing visible.

I had no idea where the missing aircraft was or what happened to it. I decided to search the auxiliary strip carefully, which I knew would stir up the security guards. I stuck a piece of duct tape over both my licence plates and went out on the runway, accelerating to over one hundred miles an hour. From canvassing this spot a year ago I knew the security guards only had a military issue six cylinder van to patrol with. I was driving one of my large eight cylinder Ford trucks, capable of close to one hundred and twenty miles an hour.

I was going flat out until I reached the apex of the V where the control tower and maintenance building were located. I slowed to make a hard right, and sped up again. I had not seen any aircraft parked, or guards following. I continued to almost the end of the runway, over three miles from the front gate which was the only way out.

That was when I spotted the Californians, parked just off the runway. I pulled in fast and started yelling instructions on unloading the plane and loading the truck. Instead of leaping to help they got hurt feeling because I did not congratulate them. This pissed me off even more. I had miles to go just to get off government property and the charges would be many years for me and these two dumbasses if we were caught here.

They were completely clueless.

After two or three minutes of frantic work I was back in the truck and racing down the middle of the runway. As I made the turn by the control tower I spotted two vehicles on the move to cut me off and prevent my escape. Needless to say, I was determined and had no intention of stopping. I had eight hundred pounds of extra weight to maneuver with and it noticeably slowed the truck. I could not round any corner at too fast a clip or risk tipping over. I dodged the guards attempts to stop me by crashing into me. I made it out the gate and turned north to Austin, one hundred and fifty miles away.

In those days before cell phones and Google maps I had a large book that covered every county in Texas. It had every small road, and even houses displayed on it. As soon as I outdistanced the security guards and shook them off my tail I turned onto a gravel road and found a place to stop out of sight. My plan was to map a circuitous route back to Austin and the stash house.

I spent time figuring out the route that would keep me off paved roads. I knew all the available cops would be looking for me. So I went east and west to travel north. It took five hours to travel that hundred and fifty miles. Every minute was crammed with paranoia but I was lucky and made the trip without seeing one cop.

**

Because of the wrecked aircraft still on that mountain in Mexico the trip was not over. The Indians were left with a sizable problem and there was nothing I could do except make suggestions on what to do with the broken airframe. I suggested a large wood fire to melt the plane, leaving nothing but a puddle of aluminum and the engine. They could bury those parts and be done with this stupid problem that could have cost all of them their lives.

The growers were a simple people who did their jobs well and hoped to be paid for the labor and risk involved. They made far more money growing pot than just growing food for their families.

I doubled their pay and got them more work, by way of a weak apology.

Chapter Twelve

By regulating the system that causes fear and anxiety in the body and brain marijuana helps to control PTSD

The Mechanics of an Airdrop

The trials and tribulations of procuring, transporting and selling marijuana.

The pilots from the debacle in the last chapter cost me dearly, and the loss of life was unacceptable. But I was deep in debt to my backers so, reluctantly, I gave those pilots one more chance and tried another airdrop. I only tried the airdrop method twice. This was the second one.

The pilots had a Helios Courier at their disposal which at that time was the best short field landing and take-off aircraft available in the world. The fact that they had access to one was the main reason I decided to try using these pilots again.

The Courier was a tail wheel equipped, high wing aircraft with a strong frame. It was made for bush pilots operating on minimal short, rough remote strips all over the world. It also performed well at altitudes of ten thousand feet or lower. It was perfect for a Mexico bound smuggling trip.

I built a landing strip in the state of Jalisco, Mexico. It was situated at an altitude of eight thousand feet and was a ten hour walk from the nearest road. I stipulated the pilots do an inspection of this construction to familiarize themselves with the length and possible obstructions before they flew.

My construction crew was at their disposal. If they needed any adjustments for their safety it would have been taken care of immediately. The pilots, just like the last time, did not want to take a two day walking trip to verify the strip. They clearly had not learned anything from their experiences. When I informed them this was a deal breaker they reluctantly agreed. After the bent prop episode this became an unbreakable rule for me. Anyone working with me had to comply or the deal was off.

The pilots made the walk and were impressed with the shape and condition of the strip, especially as it had been made without a bulldozer. My crew were paid a fat bonus for being excellent at their job.

I had paid off a different ranch for the drop in Texas. I had around twenty strips all over Texas which I used on a rotating basis, returning to each one around every fifth trip. The time between visits varied greatly, depending on what sort of trips were made each short. For this trip, the only potential problem I could see was the distance from the ranch to the number two and three backup landing strips, which were on either side of a large lake near Austin. It was an hour's drive from backup strip two to number three. The drive from the ranch to the number two backup strip was forty-five minutes.

There was one other problem, the real possibility of not having enough room inside the aircraft to fit the parachutes to the packages and still be able to safely push them out the rear cargo door. I cautioned the pilots and they said it would be an easy operation – no problem. Although I had far more experience than the Californians in smuggling, and not a great deal of faith in them, I was not familiar with small airdrops, so having made my statement I left it at that.

I had, still have, a very sensitive antenna for trouble and most of the time it is correct. Throughout my life, whenever I have paid close attention to these warnings they have kept me alive and out of many dangerous situations. Whenever I haven't there has been trouble. On this occasion, if they had been visible, I am sure my antennae would have been vibrating, so alarmed were they making me. I began making small changes to ensure success. I hired an extra driver to sit on the number two, B strip. Already, I felt sure the airdrop would not happen.

With the expectation of using the number two strip I made some changes.

The major flaw at the delivery end of this smuggling trip was the distance between the two alternative strips if the airdrop was not possible. After making the flight from Mexico the aircraft would not have enough fuel to loiter, waiting for the ground crew to reposition, and the radio was short range, no more than ten miles ground to air. The Californians were to leave from Arizona, which was closer to the Mexican airstrip, saving fuel and giving a little more range to ensure our success.

The arrangements were finalized, weather checked, and everything set for the next day. One last phone call and the smuggling trip was in motion.

The flight down was uneventful, the aircraft sound, and no problems. Because they had walked the strip the pilots had two reference points for navigation to see what was a small, hard to distinguish strip. They landed successfully, loaded the marijuana and refuelled from the plastic containers of fuel they brought with them. The take-off was flawless, with good weather and full fuel tanks and a flight range of one thousand miles. With the drop area at eight hundred miles all was set for a comfortable, easy trip.

The fight went well, and there were no problems crossing the border. But the pilots found that there wasn't enough room to outfit the packages with the parachutes, exactly as I had feared. There was also a slight headwind which reduced the range by about one hundred miles. The pilots arrived at the drop area and informed me by the short range radio that they were going to strip number two.

I raced there, thinking they would already be there by the time I arrived but the only person there was the backup driver I hired. It was getting dark fast, and the strip did not have lighting. I told the driver to wait another four hours before leaving, and raced to the number three strip, since where else could they be?

Number three strip was on top of a three or four hundred foot flat top hill. It had lighting and was in good shape. Situated as it was next to a small Texas town, it had extra protection for aircraft parked there in the form of the local police, who drove up the hill and locked the entrance gate at sunset each evening. I had checked this out and knew the routine. At sunrise they would come back and unlock the gate.

I had been using the short range ground to air radio for hours trying to raise the Californians and it was running low on battery power. I had no idea where the crew was. There were no cell phones in those days, just beepers to get back in touch. I drove to the locked gate but could not see the aircraft.

With no idea what to do next I drove to the next small town and rented a motel room. It was getting on for midnight and as dark as pitch, with no moon. I was worried they may have had a mechanical problem and been forced to land, or even crashed. I sat by my beeper in that motel room and waited. At around two in the morning the beeper finally went off, leaving a phone number. I called them from a pay phone and heard that they were at the base of the hill where the strip was located.

Running low on fuel they were forced to land and parked in the tie down area close to the gate. They saw the cop lock the gate and that made them nervous, since the airplane was stuffed with weed. Had the cop seen them and checked it they would have been busted.

Without enough fuel to go anywhere, and after waiting an hour, they taxied down the side of the strip so they parked at the opposite end to the gate and did a foot search for a spot. They found a small drainage culvert made of concrete, maybe two by two foot of space to work with. The airplane had fifteen to eighteen bales of marijuana in it. They taxied close to the culvert, unloaded, and taxied to the tie down area. Then they returned to the culvert and laboriously fill it with the weed. After that they walked down the hill and beeped me.

I drove the short distance to their location and picked them up.

The pilots filled me in on the circumstances; fuel almost exhausted, the strip lit all night, nobody on duty without a phone call. I knew this, because I had researched this strip and made it number three, the final backup. The parallels between this trip and the previous one involving them were obvious. I would never use these pilots again.

Now there was a new problem. The load was stashed on the strip and would have to be moved in the early morning before the commuter pilots arrived to make their preparations for departure. The pilots had done their job and delivered the load. The new problem fell to me.

The local cops would come to unlock the gate at just before sunrise. I was in a pickup truck parked on the route they used to get to the gate and observed them doing their job and leaving almost immediately. That was a relief, since they did not do a drive around inspecting the strip for anything unusual, say one thousand pounds of weed clogging the drainpipe.

As soon as they drove down the hill I drove through the gate to the drainpipe, and inspected the problem made by two able bodied young men, and left for me to extract alone. It was difficult to unstick the bales in any kind of a hurry and took just short of an hour. It was one of the longest hours of my life.

I left at a slow pace, just in case I had been observed. When doing something that could take ten years from your life you do not want suspicion aroused or unanswerable questions pondered. If you act like you belong and convey that impression to anyone curious enough to look it is far more likely you will be successful.

I drove slowly to San Francisco, taking almost three days to get there. On arrival I ran into a totally unexpected problem. The Government had announced Agent Orange spraying had begun in Mexico, except they called it by another name. It was falsely claimed that the entire marijuana crop out of Mexico had been sprayed and that scared the Californians who were to buy the load. They were no longer interested in purchasing any weed from Mexico. Fear tactics are always effective on Americans. If they stopped and thought about it for a second it would have been obvious it was a contrived lie. But they did not think about it, or verify by testing the product, a simple failsafe.

I sat in a Howard Johnsons Hotel in Marin County just north of San Francisco for over a month. My expense budget was used up and I had investors and workers waiting to be paid. The potential buyers were still afraid of any Mexican marijuana.

I came up with an idea on how to move this excellent and clean product. I had smoked it daily and it had no negative effect, no ill effects at all. It was clean and fresh and better than average.

I made a move and rented a seagoing steel container. I filled it with the weed, plus furniture from garage sales to cover the product, and shipped it to Hawaii. Next, I contacted my connections in Northern and Southern California and told them I had Hawaiian weed for sale. They all seemed interested in a working vacation and four or five made the trip straight away.

To my surprise, they began a bidding war and bid it up enough to cover all the extra expenses, plus a bit more.

Then they had to ship it back to California. Naturally, they passed the extra expense onto their customers. It was an excellent product and everyone involved made money and were satisfied.

The trials and tribulations of procuring, transporting and selling marijuana. It reads like fiction but it was real.

Chapter Thirteen

Marijuana protects the brain after a stroke

Background Information

What is this product that I smuggled, and why isn't it legal?

Marijuana is more than a recreational drug. It is also a medicine that can be used as a treatment and cure for an almost endless list of maladies. One of the most positive of these is that it reduces seizures, especially in young children. In addition, various forms of cancer can be treated with marijuana oil topically, or taken orally. Patients suffering from multiple sclerosis have reported reduced pain from muscle spasms after smoking marijuana. Likewise, patients with Parkinson's disease have reduced tremors, and people suffering from PTSD have reduced anxiety. For patients undergoing chemotherapy the use of marijuana helps to lessen the unpleasant side effects of nausea, vomiting, and loss of appetite.

Hemp from the marijuana plant can be (and has been for centuries) used to make clothes, rope, a carbon negative form of concrete called hempcrete, paper, hemp plastic which is more environmentally friendly, biodiesel, as a soil and water purifier, and even cosmetics, using hemp seed oil. Hemp seeds are high in protein and amino acids and can be eaten roasted, or the oil from the seeds can be used for cooking. The marijuana plant is one of the most versatile plants on the planet and has been used for multiple purposes for centuries. It is only in modern times that it has been vilified.

Unfortunately, nowadays it has been demonized to such an extent that people are afraid of it and those who use it are considered at best losers and at worst criminals. According to popular belief, it is the source of all evil. The main reason for all these attacks can be traced to 'big pharma' which is against it because if legalized worldwide, marijuana is a cheap and effective medicine. Capitalism cannot take on marijuana and win.

So, what do you do if your business models are petrified of such competition? You make it the monster in our midst, the root of every evil, and use endless excuses to lie about its influences and effects. It is classified as a schedule one drug in the United States. Schedule one drugs are those that are illegal because they have the potential for high abuse and have no medical use, and also have severe safety concerns. Narcotics such as heroin, LSD and cocaine are schedule one drugs.

Big pharma makes money by treating symptoms, not by healing. There is a great deal of material on the way big pharma manipulates information and discoveries in order to continue profiting from treating symptoms. A healthy public is not a money making public.

I find it astonishing that the abuse of alcohol is not illegal. An angry drunk is far more destructive than a person who has been smoking marijuana. Let me put it this way. Would you rather be on the road with a drunk, angry and aggressive person exceeding the speed limit, or a stoned, slow driving, peaceful person minding their own business?

Although I didn't set out that way, I ended up dedicating my life to making marijuana available, and I was lucky to fall in love with a product that turned out to be a lifesaver for many. I do not understand exactly how and why my actions in taking plants across an invisible and arbitrary line could earn me a lifetime in prison.

In the beginning I was unhappy with my government's treatment of me and my compatriots and considered the government to be derelict in its sworn duty to provide the care necessary to returning soldiers.

I wanted to strike a minor blow to undermine my government's power both in the States and in other countries. From my perspective, marijuana was a logical choice in my personal war against my government. Of course, the government was unaware of either my success or my failure. After all, if they had a clue I would definitely have been a failure.

Of course, in any life choice, there are positives and negatives, highs and lows. Nobody can have it all. I became a valued and trusted smuggler and I loved the challenging life I chose. But because of that life I alienated my wife and daughter, and became an outcast from my mother and other close relatives.

Right from the start my instincts told me the legal powers were misrepresenting all the positive attributes of marijuana, and now with the internet anyone can do their own research to find out the multiple purposes this humble plant can be used for.

Anyone caught dealing in marijuana and goes to jail becomes part of the jail system. The jail system is commercialized, a jail for profit system that can destroy three or even four generations. People who have been to jail are felons who can no longer vote. America has the largest prisoner population per capita on the planet and sixty percent of the prison population is there for smoking or selling marijuana.

I don't understand why the average American supports this, for want of a better word, criminal action against a large segment of our population. The recreational use of drugs is part of our psychological makeup. Alcohol is not illegal, yet alcohol does major damage in many ways. Alcohol fuels aggressive behavior but is tolerated.

For me, choosing to become an outlaw was a natural path. I despised my president at the time, Nixon, and was disappointed in how easily led my fellow Americans had become. They refused to question authority, abandoning their number one responsibility as citizens of the US. No man is an island; I believe that is the quote.

Outlaws lead a solitary life and give up much for what little they gain.

For me, a solitary life was preferable. Witnessing the cruelty one person is capable of, and how easy it is to justify it was eye opening and appalling to me. Our species is, for the most part, disengaged, especially with strangers.

The best traits of humanity - empathy, sympathy, just connecting - seems difficult and too easy to deny. Are we afraid of each other, or unwilling to share our rations (our wealth, our good fortune, whatever we value) with a stranger? Why have we become so distant, so suspicious of each other? My questions do not have easy answers.

Sometimes I wonder about this world I was born into, and where humanity will end up. I do make moves to help others as often as the chance presents itself. At times it works and at others, nada.

Perhaps my chosen career was not profound. Planning and executing operations and sticking your finger in the authority figure's eye are certainly not profound. Looking back, my fundamental reason for smuggling is difficult to pinpoint. Was it the thrill and the adventure? Or maybe it was the knowledge that this was something I could do that others couldn't. It could have been the freedom that came with not having a regular job. Then there was the breath-taking scenery I was privy to on my trips and on the side trips I took to some amazing places. There was my belief that my government treated returning soldiers shamefully, and that the war in Vietnam should not have happened. And finally, there was the conviction that marijuana should never have been made illegal and I was making my stand, however small. I guess, in the end, it was a bit of all of that.

One thing is certain; I had many adventures and this book is only a tiny fragment of them. In the pipeline is further installments in the roller coaster ride that was marijuana smuggling.

What I have Learned from this Life

Early Chinese doctors used marijuana as an anesthetic by reducing the plant powder and mixing it with wine for administration before surgery. The Chinese term for "anesthesia" (mázui 麻醉) literally means "cannabis intoxication"

Being a drug smuggler, as it's portrayed in numerous movies and television series, is a free and easy life with plenty of money and women. The reality is far removed from this.

The reality of successful drug smuggling is a life that is often lonely. A high profile is not recommended if you want to be successful, stay successful, and stay alive. There are lengthy periods of time spent alone, and when you are with people they are frequently the dangerous kind which requires you to stay alert and think twice before you speak. It's a stressful life interspersed with periods of boredom.

And yet, I experienced personal growth that I would not have had in any other occupation. The old me was smart, but perhaps self obsessed and shallow, although I like to think I was always kind and considerate to my fellow human beings.

Following is some of the ways I changed during my years of drug smuggling, and how I have come to call myself a living example, my name being associated with drug smuggling and prison.

Back when it all started I was advised by someone I looked up to as a role model not to go to war with my government. I agreed, but could not resist the urge to prick

Nixon as much as I could. Nixon was disgusted with my generation, and my chosen product. He declared war on drugs, on marijuana. That was so many shades of ridiculous. How can you wage war on a substance?

I didn't go to war with my government, not in an obvious way. I chose to smuggle marijuana, sometimes by the tons.

Not long into my career I was busted in the state of Guerrero, Mexico, and received a sentence that was four times the normal number of years. That was thanks to a bribe paid by my government to all federal Mexican judges. It amounted to fifty thousand dollars per month, per judge, so long as they did the bidding of Dick Nixon.

That should have been the end of my career but it wasn't, and after a few months I engineered my escape. The uproar in Mexico that followed my escape led to a gang being sent to kill me before I got home. But I made it home. That is why I call myself a Living Example. I could be wrong of course.

***

When I first began smuggling marijuana I had very little knowledge or understanding of the Mexican culture. I did speak a few words of Spanish but had foolishly not taken Spanish classes when in grade school. It was a silly attitude but one typical of most Texas residents, even though we share a border with Mexico. A denial of reality perhaps.

In Mexico I felt like a stranger in a strange land. The speed at which a Mexican national speaks is fast, even the poorly educated. They use a lot of slang, which confused me even further.

Aside from the language barrier there was a cultural barrier, on my side at any rate as I had little understanding of the Mexican culture.

In the early seventies, when I began my career, the Mexican families protected the women, especially the younger ones. They could not leave the home without supervision. Courtship took place on a Sunday afternoon, usually in the courtyard of the local church. The older women of the family kept an eagle eye on their young charges. The women I saw running errands on the streets were between fifty and seventy years old, all with a shawl wrapped around their heads and upper body. This was all totally foreign to me and I found it puzzling. But it was not my place to challenge the culture of another country. Music and the dress code have freed the younger Mexican women, but still they are ridiculed on the streets for wearing trousers. They are strong willed, these young Mexican women, and they ignore the strong reactions from their more conservative parents and grandparents. They could be considered living examples themselves, perhaps. People showing strength like a young Mexican woman wearing trousers in public.

I was surprised by the open attitudes towards me by the Mexican people. I was a young man in my early twenties, empty headed, but the Mexicans I came into contact with showed me respect and looked to me for ideas. I had no idea why and it felt strange to be afforded this respect. It wasn't until I overhead conversations in English between educated Mexicans about the fact that humanity, and Americans in particular, had walked on the moon that I realized why I was getting so much undeserved respect. Understanding why I became a bit more comfortable with it, but the oversized amount of respect I got never sat well with me.

Everyday things like driving presented a challenge, with the road rules so different. When I came to a stop sign or a corner I automatically hit the brakes. The other, Mexican driver would see me slow and would speed up, going through the intersection in front of me. The basic rule to driving in Mexico was he who hesitates is lost – very macho in this male oriented country.

In the countryside there were many single lane bridges. The rule was not to wait your turn. The rule was to approach the bridge at sixty plus miles an hour and turn on your headlights. The driver who was first to do so owned the bridge and would speed up, racing for the bridge regardless of what you did. If you met on the bridge it was expected that the driver who was last to turn on his lights was the one to back up.

Over the years more road signs have been posted on the major roads, plus stop signs and signs giving the distance to destinations. There are also more signs explaining who has the right of way. This more organized approach caused chaos when first implemented and the number of accidents increased for several years, until the drivers adjusted to the more controlled environment.

The overall feel and look of this country was exotic, and the smells in the air foreign. The food was strange, but after exposure I embraced Mexican cuisine wholeheartedly.

But that was the surface, underneath it was the poverty. I had never seen true poverty before and it had a profound impact on my view of our world. I witnessed a degree of poverty I had little idea existed. Every stream I passed had several women pounding their laundry clean on rocks. I was amazed at the difference between our rich lifestyle and the poverty stricken structure of Mexican life.

Over the years the Mexican way of life has improved. A few years after I began my career almost everyone had a small washing machine and women's lives became less demanding. Set in their ways, the older Mexicans resented the changes going on around them but some of them adapted and they are the living examples.

***

My experiences helped me to grow as a person, to become stronger and sharper, but also to become more empathetic and kind. Here are some ways in which my lifestyle changed me and the lessons I learned:

Relatability: It was a free flowing atmosphere. I had to be open to what was necessary, fine tune things and make changes while in constant motion. The wrong move would cause both myself and others to suffer immediate consequences. My judgment was trusted and my suggestions always considered and in most cases followed. This had the effect on me of increasing my self-worth and sharpening my decision making processes.

Intrigue: Unseen forces were arrayed against me and my compatriots, put in motion to thwart my attempts to move my product north. They were unscrupulous and at times vicious and even death dealing. I had to keep my wits about me at all times and this sharpened my sense of danger.

Empathy: I have always been empathetic, but the wrong decision in this life had the potential to cost a friend his or her freedom or life. For that reason I did as many of the operations involved myself as I could. I bought the product, flew it in and sold it myself. I did my operation with four people, no less, and that meant I put three others at the minimal amount of risk as possible by taking on as much of it as I could. The responsibility weighed on me and today I do tend to feel responsible for all who come into my circle. I don't see this as a bad thing.

Likability: In my career, likability was an asset. If people liked you they were more inclined to trust you and to give you the benefit of the doubt. If a mistake was made I changed direction to correct it and I had a high success rate. Those few who knew me were willing to do almost anything for my success because they knew I would be there for them if necessary. My success was their success, shared. With mutual respect everyone involved does their best to backup all participants and that went a long way to assuring the success of a trip.

Perspective: We are all limited by our learned views on subjects we know little about. It is a lifelong struggle to keep up, learn more, know more, so the perspective is true.

Other people: We all judge through the eyes of consumer based assumptions. Present as neat and tidy, drive an acceptable vehicle, look trustworthy and people are more likely to believe they can deal with you.

Relating to others: Some people have difficulty relating to any other people, and that often is the result of how they were treated by those they were close to. Expect to have some people dislike you and don't take it personally.

Do what it takes to succeed except one: This one is simple and should be the basis for every operation undertaken by every person. If your success depends on doing some sort of damage to friends or family you should rethink it and change your direction. Think about how different the world would be if everyone used this as the basis for decision making.

Setting goals: In my experience, the old wives tale is true: be careful what you wish for because you might get it.

Personal view: Everyone has ego struggles. Get over yourselves and get on with it. Simple.

Personal limitations: If you are unaware of your limitations seek advice from a close friend or relative who may have a different view on your direction. Sometimes they will see what you do not. Act on personal limitations to stretch them.

***

In this journey of my life, this real life movie, the real victims are the people marijuana has the potential to help. People who have a medical need, plus the non-medical and non-hallucinogenic uses that could make such a difference to our every day lives, that's the end losers.

I wanted to do something to thwart my government, and I strongly believe that marijuana has been given an unfair label as the devil's substance. Marijuana can grow just about anywhere if you broadcast the seeds. It grows quickly and can be used for many different purposes. People who gravitate to this product tend to be harder to control and less likely to believe everything propaganda tells them.

Criminalizing marijuana is jail for profit, and up to four generations suffer, to fill jails and end the voting rights of these people, who may be the enemy of capitalism.

The lead character of this movie, me, became more certain I was right and more determined to keep the pressure up. I doubled down on my mission to make my product available to all adults who were interested. Meanwhile, the government firmed on the decision to eradicate the people involved with the procurement and transportation of marijuana. The ending for me was each successful smuggling trip and the beginning of the next one, my own, more positive version of capitalism.

The more the government insisted marijuana was bad the more stubborn I was and the more determined I was to provide weed to the general public, and thwart all attempts by the powers that be to imprison, and or harm me in other ways.

The end of this movie? Well, it's taken fifty years to play out and the ending is still not sure. I was so naïve in the beginning. I thought marijuana would be legalized by 1972. Here we are, and while it is legal in some places it is still a forbidden substance in many more.

Humankind must question authority, question those sacred cows, support each other, or be defeated.

***

My story is not over and I am still fighting the fight against authority. The tales you have been reading may sound like I made them up but they are all true, and there are many more. The story of my escape from Acapulco has only been touched on in this book, and will be gone into in more depth in my next book, *Escape from Acapulco.* Follow me on Amazon to be sent a notification when it is released.

My final piece of advice to you, the reader is this: Be open, be aware, make informed decisions, follow your own path, and above all be kind.

92294855R00088

Made in the USA
Lexington, KY
01 July 2018